MO]

ALICE TAYLOR

'There is no writer more full of the milk of human kindness.'
Books Ireland

'In Ireland ... she has become the most popular and universally
loved author in memory.' *Mail on Sunday*

'Taylor [has a] remarkable gift of elevating the ordinary to something
special, something poetic, even ... She is a teller of stories, simply
that. She writes from personal experience and records the experience of others, without the gravitas and authority of an historian, but
with empathy, wit and considerable poetic elegance.' *Irish Independent*

'Ireland's Laurie Lee ... a chronicler of fading village life
and rural rituals.' *The Observer*

'Taylor's telling makes the world of her village universal, and sets her
firmly in that mysteriously potent Irish storytelling tradition.'
Los Angeles Times

'People read Alice Taylor's books, people crave Alice Taylor's
company because they want to find peace. They find it in the leaves
of her books and the folds of her laughter.' *Ireland on Sunday*

About the Author

Alice Taylor's books have become
international bestsellers in many
languages: her series of memoirs
of Irish country life also includes
To School through the Fields, *The
Women*, *Do You Remember?*, *Quench
the Lamp* and *The Village*. She
is the author of two bestselling
novels, *The Woman of the House*
and *Across the River*.

FOR A COMPLETE LIST, SEE WWW.OBRIEN.IE

ALICE TAYLOR

Country Days

BRANDON

To Ellen, for days in the attic

This edition first published 2016 by
Brandon, an imprint of The O'Brien Press Ltd
12 Terenure Road East, Rathgar,
Dublin 6, D06 HD27, Ireland.
Tel: +353 1 4923333; Fax: +353 1 4922777
E-mail: books@obrien.ie
Website: www.obrien.ie
Originally published 1993.

The O'Brien Press is a member of Publishing Ireland.

ISBN: 978-1-84717-874-9

1 3 5 7 8 6 4 2
16 18 20 21 19 17

Printed and bound by Norhaven Paperback A/S, Denmark.
The paper in this book is produced using pulp from managed forests

Contents

NANNA'S CORSET

I SAUNTERED SLOWLY along the dusty road, kicking loose stones ahead of me. It was a warm day, and I felt as languid as the black and yellow bumble bee droning on the hedge beside me. I sat down on the side of the ditch and watched a ladybird crawl up my bare brown leg. I was on my way to spend a week with my grandmother and was reluctant to arrive.

Every summer my mother encouraged each one of us to spend a week with our grandmother, but as she was a strict disciplinarian who believed that children should behave as adults, I preferred to be at home where the pace was more leisurely. Reluctant as I was, my mother exercised her emotional blackmail about "poor lonely Nanna", and even though I did not believe one word of it, I still found myself headed in her direction.

Dawdle as I might, I could not drag out the journey any longer and arrived as my uncle was herding the cows into the stalls for milking.

The kitchen of the long, low thatched house was cool after the hot sun outside. As soon as I arrived in the doorway, my grandmother handed me a white enamel bucket with instructions to go out and collect the eggs.

"Poor lonely Nanna, my eye," I thought.

I lined the bottom of the bucket with a handful of hay to prevent breakages and carefully placed the eggs on top of each other. One side of the white-washed henhouse was lined with timber perches, while on the other side a variety of different containers, ranging from rusty tar barrels to orange boxes, served as laying nests.

Balancing my bucket carefully, I took it back to the kitchen, where the next task was cleaning the eggs with a damp cloth and bread-soda. At home this job could be put off to the next day and then the chances were that someone else could get caught for it, but here there was no such luck. Then I had to tidy the kitchen and set the table for the helpers coming in from the milking.

Afterwards I wandered around the deserted farmyard chasing the wild cats in and out through the stable windows. They lived in the straw loft untouched by human hand and they had no children to play with them. My grandmother did not allow them near the kitchen, so they were fed by my uncle in a rusty churn cover after morning and evening milking. Going back into the haggard behind the house, I climbed up into the old apple tree, lay out along one of the branches and looked up at the late evening sky through the different shapes made by the dark green leaves and the big red sour cooking apples that this tree produced by the bucketful.

In the gathering dusk, my grandmother rapped on the back window of the kitchen, summoning me in to go to bed. I shared her big feather bed that smelt of Sloan's Liniment and camphor balls. I whipped off my short cotton dress, dragged on my nightdress and jumped into the soft down. She hauled me back out to scrub myself in cold water and to kneel down and say my prayers.

Matthew, Mark, Luke and John,

Bless the bed that I lie on,

And if I die before I wake

The Lord I give my soul to take.

When I had my night prayers said, I crept back into bed. I lay there and watched her nightly ritual.

First she wound her clock. It had weights and chains, and she pulled down the chains which made a whirring sound as the weights climbed upwards. Then she took off her black bonnet and hung it off the brass knob at the end of the bed. Next the crotchet shawl from around her shoulders was carefully placed over the curved back of a leather-seated chair. Her long black apron she untied and folded across the seat of the chair. Then she eased open the buttons down the front of her black satin blouse. There were two long rows of tiny satin-covered buttons to be opened, so it took some time as her fingers moved slowly from one to the other, feeling her way along as she looked out the window across the fields. She commented on the condition of the countryside and the evening sky and forecast tomorrow's weather as a result of her observations.

She draped the blouse over the shoulders of the chair. She untied the waist of her long black skirt; it slid to the floor and she stepped out of it. Carefully she folded its pleats and arranged it across the chair seat over the apron. Now she stood resplendent in a long-sleeved white chemise and flowing red petticoat. I always felt that it was a pity to cover that flaming red petticoat, but somehow I could never imagine my grandmother sporting it anywhere other than in the privacy of her own bedroom. Next the petticoat crumpled in crimson folds at her feet and was picked up to be folded carefully over the skirt. A large navy blue knickers stretched from her waist to the top of her black stockings. She eased up its gathered elasticated legs and snapped open the suspenders of her whalebone corset: three suspenders for each leg, two to the back and one to the front. Then she drew down one side of her knickers and clicked the corset open down along that side, and I counted the clicks as she went along. There was an almost musical rhythm to the clicking, and I challenged myself every night to get my count of the last of the clicks to coincide with the grand finale when she finally whipped it off with a clatter of bone and steel against the iron leg of the bed.

She sat on the side of the bed to unlace her high black boots, which she placed carefully side by side under her chair; then she rolled down her long, black, knitted stockings. After this her chemise was arched up over her head and a yellow bodice came into view.

The final unveiling was hidden from my eyes as she opened the door of the tall wardrobe and it swung between us. It had a mirror on the door, and so I saw myself behind the black bars of the bed. When she stepped from behind it, she was dressed from neck to toe and wrist in a flowing nightgown.

With each layer she removed, she had become less formidable, and when she undid her long grey hair that she wore coiled on top of her head, it flowed down over her shoulders. She was then transformed from my regal grandmother to a tall, waif-like figure. She peeled the bedclothes back at her side of the bed and sat propped up by large feather pillows. Even though we shared the same bed, I was on a lower plateau as she reposed high above me on a mountain of pillows. She said the rosary and many prayers and taught me one of them. For many nights we laboured over that prayer, and I thought that it was the longest prayer I had ever heard.

Dear angel ever at my side
How loving thou must be,
To leave thy home in heaven above
And guard a little child like me...

There were twenty-six more lines. It was broken up into verses – at least that's what I considered them to be – and we took a verse per night. Finally, from the sheer power of repetition, she drummed it into my sleepy head. As I learned, my drowsy mind could visualise a huge angel with coloured wings sitting on the brass bars at the bottom of the bed.

She was different then from the daytime grand-mother. She told stories of her girlhood and traced the family tree with great detail. I fell asleep to the sound of her voice getting fainter as I dozed off.

My grandmother was a late riser, so I got up early the following morning and escaped before she had a chance to line up jobs for me. My aim was to visit Molly, who lived across the fields. During her meanderings the night before, my grandmoth-er had mentioned that Molly had a grandnephew from America staying with her. I put my ears back at this bit of news and on asking for further details was dismissed with the remark that he was "a nice looking child". In my grandmother's book, a child could range from a baby to a twenty-year-old, so I was soon on my way to investigate this visitor from foreign parts.

I came on him suddenly, where he lay stretched out on the headland of the meadow, peering through the tall grass and watching the baby rabbits intently.

"Hi," he said in surprise, "who are you?"

"Who are you?" I countered.

"I'm Shane," he said, "and I think that I know who you are because yesterday Aunty Molly said you were coming. Gee, you are pretty!" he finished in surprise.

When you are thirteen and you consider your mouth to be too big, your hair too straight and your legs too long, anybody who tells you that you are pretty opens a door into a whole new exciting world. When that somebody happened to be male, dark and good looking, it was music to my soul.

As I gazed down at him, stretched out on the grass, I tried to judge if he was as tall as I was. It would be bad for my morale if he had to look up at me.

"Will you stand up?" I asked him.

"Sure," he said in surprise, jumping to his feet.

"Now stand still," I instructed and stood with my back against his, reaching up with my hand to judge our head levels.

"You're an inch ahead," I told him.

"Is that important?" he asked.

"Yes," I told him. "I don't like short boys."

"Well, glad I passed the test," he said, looking a bit perplexed; "and now will we watch the rabbits?"

The rabbits, however, had disappeared from view. We spent the rest of the morning creeping silently over rusty gates and across mossy ditches to take the rabbits by surprise and then watch them scamper in all directions when they saw us. Shane was fascinated by the rabbits and I was fascinated by Shane. His black curly hair fell forward over his eyes and he had a habit of running his long, slender fingers through it to comb it backwards. When he laughed, golden flecks seemed to sparkle in his brown eyes. He laughed a lot and was thrilled and delighted with things that I considered everyday and ordinary. Being with him was full of laughter and fun.

When we got thirsty from the heat of the sun, we crawled down into a deep stream and drank the water by cupping it into our saucered fists. I introduced Shane to birds' nests, and he was like a miner who had struck gold: there was no satisfying his quest for more. Some of the nests had eggs in them, but his ambition now was to find one that had baby birds. Although we searched many ditches and bushes, no nest sheltering young came our way. As we searched we talked. His conversation was full of words that I had never heard before, and he asked me to explain some of my ways of saying things to him. We had a great time trying to understand each other, and I loved his drawling American accent.

Finally it dawned on me that it was well into the afternoon and that my grandmother would be on the rampage, so I brought Shane back with me as an insurance policy against a sermon. The ploy worked because even though she might have felt like wigging my ear, she could not do so without including Shane in the hostilities, and he was after all a visitor. More important still, he was Molly's grandnephew and Molly was her dearest friend.

The following day, hay was drawn in from the meadows to the barn by horse and float. Shane and I sat under the warm galvanised-iron roof of the hay barn and watched a swallow swish in to feed her young in her mud-encrusted nest perched high in the corner of the arching rafter. She waited until the horse and float left the haggard before she swooped in, snails dangling from her small, sharp beak.

We had gone for drives in the float, bumping around on its hard surface on the way out and coming home legs trailing along the ground at the back. Our bare toes were soothed by the soft grass brushing along beneath us, with the occasional thistle causing us to whip up our damaged legs in agony. Shane had never before gone barefoot and he hooted with delight at the feel of the cool moss beneath his feet.

We were supposed to be helping, lifting up the hay at the base of the load to ease the float in and sometimes packing hay at the back of the barn. But all that day we watched the swallow and hoped that the hay would rise high enough for us to reach its nest.

While the block of hay was low, we could not see into the nest and could only watch as the mother's head disappeared in over the edge and her tail bobbed up and down while she dished out delicacies to her young. Gradually the block of hay rose higher as the horse drew home load after load, and finally late in the evening our straining fingers could touch the rough timber rafters. We gathered together armfuls of crackling hay and piled it high to bridge the gap between us and the roof. Shane climbed on to the top of the wobbling hay and swung up on to the rafters. I balanced on the peak of the wavering heap and reached towards the hands straining down to pull me up. Grasping long brown fingers, I clambered up beside him on to the warm wooden rafters and leaned forward on all fours to maintain my balance. Care had to be exercised to prevent wooden splinters digging deep into knees and palms. He crept along before me towards the nest. Our rafter crawl took us clear of the hay, and then we were high over the empty space between the hay blocks. I was afraid to look down in case I would slip off the narrow timber and crash on to the float below. It was empty now, propped up on its timber handles, the traces draping across the shafts between which the horse had strained all day, carrying back the wynds from the meadow. We were crawling along with one thought in mind, to peep into the nest and see the baby swallows.

We were rewarded with a flash of yellow gaping beaks as we wobbled, precariously straining forward, wanting to see as much as possible but afraid of losing our balance. Then we reversed back along the rafter and collapsed back down on to the bouncing hay. Shane was delighted to have seen the baby birds and that night he drew sketches of them in the copy book that my grandmother kept behind the clock to keep a record of the egg money.

We spent every day together, and the compulsory week at my grandmother's stretched into a voluntary month, during which time we explored the countryside and talked for hours, comparing our different worlds. Going to bed at night and watching Nanna unclicking her whalebone corset, I longed for morning so that we could be together again. We were children on the last rung of childhood, reluctant to take the first step into the unknown world of adolescence.

The day he went away, I went up into the hay barn and burrowed deep down under the hay to cry in private and heal the pain of his going. Remembering the swallows, I climbed up to look into the nest. It was empty; the baby birds had flown away. That night, as Nanna's corset hit the leg of the iron bed with a clatter of bone and steel, I wondered if she had ever been young.

Old Jugs

Her room is full
Of old jugs,
Rose-patterned
Stone and lustre,
And in them
Are faded letters,
A soft baby shoe,
Key of a house
Where once she lived.
They are the
Urns of her life.
And she will
Go to sleep
Here in her
Attic room
Surrounded by her
Old jugs.

A Friend

S HE STOOD OUTSIDE the circle of chattering schoolgirls with a calm smile on her face. It was the first day of term, and while the rest of the girls were busy getting to know each other, she was content to wait and let things happen. She was creamy skinned and curly haired, with pale blue eyes that almost disappeared when her face crinkled into lines of laughter. When you talked to her, Eileen gave you her undivided attention and made you feel that everything you said was important, even to the extent of sometimes repeating your last words as if they gave her food for thought. During the following year together in that boarding school, we became good friends. She was a pleasant, easy-going companion who saw good in all of us, and life around her was a pool of serenity.

After school she went back to farming, specialising in chicken and egg production. We still kept in contact as I was working in a town not far from where she lived. I sometimes stayed with her for weekends in the family home. It was a big farmhouse with high ceilings and a wide front hall from which double glass doors opened into a glass porch, so that the front of the house always seemed to be filled with light. There was no mother in the home as she had died when they were children, which maybe made Eileen more mature than I was, even though we were about the same age. It was an old house and in the spacious bedrooms upstairs the beds were also old; in the room we shared, our bed had a sag in the middle. First into the bed slept in the sag and the other one slept on the surrounding hillside. Because we were young and flexible, the bed with the built-in dip in the middle was the cause of amusement rather than insomnia. When we came in late at night from dates and dances, we chatted and laughed at all the things that are funny when you are footloose and fancy free, and when we closed our eyes in the small hours of the morning, the humpy mattress was no barrier to sleep.

When I married a few years later I got buried in the baby bucket, as sometimes happens to young mothers, and we lost contact. I heard that she had got married, and then one day out of the blue she called with a quiet-voiced, smiling man and two little girls. It was great to see her and you had only to look at her to know that she was happy. The next time she called, there was a little boy with the two girls in the back of the car. We did not write to each other or even send each other Christmas cards, but still I would have considered her one of my dearest friends.

Then one day I met a man from her parish who told me that her husband had cancer. At the time he was in remission and the whole parish were praying for a miracle. Eileen's husband was, he told me, a man around whom their whole parish revolved, involved in the GAA, in farming organisations, in race meetings and in everything that went on in the local area. The neighbour said to me, "If you had a problem in the morning, John would be the first man in your door."

That night I rang Eileen and we talked for a long time. She was hopeful and fearful. It had gone on for almost a year, and when John took a step forward it was sometimes counteracted by two steps backwards. Just then he was going through a good patch, so hope was beginning to kindle in her heart. Shortly after that a nun from our old school died and we met at the funeral. I was delighted to meet them, and John looked so well that you would have given him a certificate of good health. It did not continue like that, however, and treatment became necessary again. From then on it was an up-and-down process with regular stays in hospital. Through it all, prayer was a great comfort to Eileen and John, and the neighbours sat with John in the hospital and called to see Eileen regularly. They had a very good friend in Fr Tom, who often said mass in John's room in the hospital and prayed with Eileen and the children at home.

During those weeks I never called to Eileen's home

or visited John in the hospital. I had not been part of their life before this illness and becoming part of it now would be an intrusion. My bond of friendship had been with Eileen herself, and our telephone conversations during those long, pain-filled days made me realise that our thinking was still in harmony. I regretted that we had lost contact over the years, that her children were now strangers to me and her much-loved husband somebody whom I had only met on a few occasions. I could be of no comfort to them now. Only close friends can help you in times of great pain.

The weekend before Christmas I was away from home, returning late on Saturday night. On the Sunday morning the phone rang and a young voice said, "I'm Eileen's daughter; Daddy is being buried today." The soft young voice was full of controlled pain, and when I put down the phone, there was an ache in my heart for my friend whom I knew would be filled with a deep sorrow.

We drove out to their parish church where the crowds overflowed on to the road outside. As there was no way we could get in, we decided to drive ahead to the graveyard which was a few miles away. Cars were parked all along the road and people huddled in the cold under the trees beside the high graveyard wall. As sometimes happens at funerals, the woman waiting beside me turned out to be an old neighbour from where I had lived as a child and who was now married on a farm near Eileen. We chatted as we waited for the funeral and she talked about Eileen and John and what great neighbours they were and how pleasant it was to be living near them. When the hearse arrived, people poured out of surrounding cars and you would wonder where the long stream of funeral cars were going to park, but everybody found a place eventually.

Eileen was pale-faced and alert and surprised me by being totally in touch with everything and everybody present. She was amazingly composed, and I thought of that young girl outside the convent so many years before. She still had her pool of serenity. As I walked past her in the row of sympathisers, she pressed my hand and whispered, "Come back to the house afterwards."

I had never been to her house. The narrow country roads in the hills behind the graveyard were not the easiest to negotiate and several times we went astray. In the end my husband suggested, "Why not leave it for another day? She would appreciate a call more in the days to come."

It was a practical suggestion, but sometimes practical suggestions are not always the ones we want to hear. We continued and finally we came in sight of the house, which was across the valley from us and on the side of a sloping hill. The yard and the road up to it were lined with cars. There was something very sad about the sight of all those cars gathered around that hillside farmhouse on a bleak December afternoon. It was a celebration of sadness, and the man who had gathered them all together was gone from their midst. I felt that Eileen was now floundering in a great solitary sea of loneliness, although surrounded by friends and neighbours.

In a farmhouse if you are a regular caller you go in the back door and if not you go to the front one. I went to the front. Inside Eileen was surrounded by people.

"I was expecting you," she said, and I sensed then that even though I would come often in the future, it was right to be there on that day. The house was packed with people and I was glad to meet Eileen's brothers and sister, some of whom I had not met since I had stayed with them years before. Neighbouring women laid out table after table of food and everybody was catered for. As Eileen and I sat together having tea late that evening, I said, looking at the laden table in front of us, "How did you get all this together?"

"Every Christmas cake in the parish is on that table today," she told me.

It was a few days before Christmas and the statement was simply made, but it told a lot about her neighbours. After the tea I asked Eileen where Fr Tom was, and she smiled and said, "Out in the back kitchen washing cups."

I found him there, and because everybody was after their tea, we had time to talk. He was a young man full of the love of God and his fellow human beings and a conversation with him overflowed with laughter. He was not a heavy-duty cleric but a heavenly violin and God's music played easily though him.

Among the topics of conversation we ranged over was the improvement in rural houses.

"I remember," he said, "when I was a child that most of the chairs in our kitchen were without backs. They had fallen off over the years, and we children sat on the backless ones and left the good chairs for the adults. One day I had to go into town to get the vet for a sick cow. I was very young and had never been in town on my own before and had a fierce job in finding his house. The wife answered the door and put me into the sitting-room. I felt that I had better not take up a good chair, so I sat on one that had no back. The wife came in and told me to sit over on another chair. But I clung to my own chair, crippled with shyness, and said that I was fine on this one. She got very annoyed and said, 'That's not a chair; that's the coffee table.'"

Fr Tom laughed as he remembered, and I said, "Far away from coffee tables a lot of us were reared."

"Yes," he said, "but all that does not matter if the heart is in the right place."

In the months that followed, any time that I rang Eileen or visited her, she had callers. The neighbours were in constant attendance and somebody called every night. During the day the farm still had to be run and it was now her sole responsibility. It worried her that she might not be able to cope, but after the first few hesitant months she came to grips with it. She had dark, anguish-filled days, but she had great faith, and prayer was her constant companion. In the evenings when the cows had been milked, she spent hours working in the garden and found healing in the earth. But it was the neighbours who were her greatest support. She was lucky to be living in a part of the country where the rural community put their arms around her and helped to make her grief more bearable.

It meant a lot to both of us that our paths had crossed again. We would keep in touch in the future because friendship, like everything valuable in life, needs a certain amount of care.

SOMEWHERE TO LAY MY HEAD

THE PHONE RANG as I came down the stairs. I picked it up to be met by an ominous silence, but when I strained my ear I could hear bronchial breathing. A jagged, hollow cough which sounded as if it was coming from the bottom of a barrel wheezed into my ear, and I knew then that it was the Major. A very old, retired British army man, over six foot tall, bottle-thin and upright, with a high bald head and a purple nose, he lived outside the village in the restored corner of an old ruined castle. There was still a pregnant silence on the phone, and I could sense that he was cranking up his ancient vocal cogs as he prepared to grind his crackling voice into action. After a certain amount of spluttering "ahum, ahum", he suddenly hiccuped into top gear.

"Alice!" he barked.

"Yes, Major," I answered. I felt like saluting smartly, clicking my heels together and adding "all present and correct".

"That confounded parcel," he growled. "Who the blazes sent me that?"

As far as the Major was concerned, nothing of any

importance had left the post office that morning except his parcel.

"No idea," I assured the Major.

"Good God!" he spluttered. "Do you mean to tell me that you have no idea who sent it?"

"No idea at all," I told him.

I was keeping my side of the conversation to a minimum because the Major had the happy knack of tying you up in knots without even trying.

"Have you any idea what's in it?" he demanded.

"No," I told him.

"Well, it's not mine," he assured me.

I decided then that I would chance a question to sort things out, with the hope that our parcel enquiry would not wander too far off the point.

"How did you get it so?" I asked.

"Damned if I know," he spluttered.

"Who is it addressed to?" I pursued.

"'The Mayor'," he announced.

"Well, that explains it," I assured him.

"Explains what?" he barked.

"The names are so alike that they got mixed up, and that is how you got it."

"Preposterous," he spluttered. "You should have sent the confounded thing to the Mayor."

"But we have no Mayor, Major," I told him, feeling that I was getting my Majors and Mayors in a tangle. The Major always succeeded in getting everyone around him confused while he blustered on, oblivious to the situation.

"And why haven't we got a Mayor?" he demanded.

Though he had lived here for years the Major knew absolutely nothing about the ordinary life of the village and it would not have surprised him in the least if he had discovered that we had a nudist colony in the Catholic church. He was convinced that we were all slightly odd and we returned the compliment.

"Well, Major, it was just a case of the names getting mixed up," I told him, "so you can give the parcel back to the postman in the morning."

"Bloody will not," he asserted. "I'm sending it back right now. Not keeping that chappie in the house overnight."

I decided then that he was mixing up the postman and the parcel, so did not pursue the subject and was glad to put down the phone.

I promptly forgot all about the Major's parcel until that night when Gabriel came into the kitchen with a strange look on his face and a small, square parcel in his hand.

"You'll never believe what's in this," he said, placing the parcel carefully on the table.

"Not another one," I protested and I went over and peered down at the writing on the parcel.

"Oh, that's the Major's parcel," I said.

"How do you know about it?" he asked in surprise.

"Well, he was on the phone, meandering on about what was in it," I answered.

"I'm not surprised that he was, the poor old devil,"

Gabriel said sympathetically.

"Well, what the hell is in there anyway?" I demanded, wondering what on earth it was all about.

"Have a look," I was invited.

I picked up the little brown box, which was surprisingly light and was wrapped neatly in strong brown paper. It had already been carefully opened, so I folded back the paper and lifted up the top of the box and peered in.

Inside was a human skull.

"Mother of God!" I gasped and dropped the box on to the table where it toppled over, spilling the skull out on to the tablecloth.

"Where in the name of God did that come from?" I yelled, staring mesmerised at the skull that sat grinning up at me. Admittedly it was a long time since it had seen active service. But I could well understand then why the Major did not want to keep "that chappie" in the house overnight. He was less confused than I had thought.

"Oh, put him back in, please," I implored. "I don't like looking at him; he's making me nervous."

"There's a message with him," Gabriel informed me calmly.

"Where is it?" I asked weakly.

Gabriel rummaged in the empty box, but found nothing.

"Oh, my God!" I said. "I think it's inside in him." The corner of a letter was sticking out through the gaping mouth.

"It must have fallen into the head," he said, promptly picking it up and extricating the note out through the gaping mouth, as if it were a letter box. I took the note gingerly and smoothed it out. It was written in very spindly writing and was difficult to read. At the top was a German address and the message was in very broken English, but the gist of the story was that the writer was a medical student who had been on holidays the previous summer in Kinsale and had visited Innishannon. He had explored our old graveyard at the end of the village and had taken a skull out of one of the tombs, thinking that it might assist him with his medical studies. He had carried the skull home with him, and then his problems had begun. Things, he related, had started to go wrong in his life and he had an accident; now he believed that the removal of the skull was the cause of all his worries. He wanted to return it, and in the accompanying note he gave details as to where he had found it, and he asked that somebody would follow his directions and replace the skull. He knew nobody in Innishannon and he assumed that the Mayor would know what to do. Like the Major, I now wished that we had a Mayor in the village.

"What are we going to do with it?" I appealed to Gabriel.

"Well, it's dark now, so it's too late to do anything," I was told.

"But where will we keep it tonight?" I wanted to know.

Before we could decide on temporary storage arrangements, the door opened and my friend Frances sailed into the kitchen. When she saw our friend on the table, a look of amazement came over her face.

"I see you have company for dinner," she remarked quizzically.

"Will you shut up," I said. "I don't think that it's a bit funny."

"Well, you'll have to admit," she said, picking up the skull without a bother on her, "that he is an unusual visitor. Aren't you, old boy?" she added, inspecting him quite fondly.

"Don't you mind handling him?" I asked.

"Not at all," she said. "We had a full one of these" – by which I think she meant a full skeleton – "in the nurses' home. We used to hang him up behind the door after study."

"Dear God," I said, "aren't I glad that I never became a nurse."

Under the influence of Frances's relaxed approach to our friend on the table, my attitude towards him was beginning to thaw out a little. I thrust the accompanying letter into her hand, and as she read it her eyes widened in surprise and she gave a low whistle.

"Interesting! Interesting," she commented. "That will teach him that an Irishman can be dangerous even when he is dead!"

"Where should we put him for the night?" I wondered.

"Take him to bed with you," Frances suggested with a wicked grin.

"God, but you are nasty," I told her.

"Put him on the kitchen window," Frances suggested then. "The dogs could get him in the yard and the cat could get him under the table, but he'll be quite safe on the window sill."

I was not sure if I found her practicality reassuring or revolting. But we put the parcel on the window and it looked quite harmless there. It could have been a box of chocolates.

"Let's give him a name," Frances decided. "It would make the whole business far more civilised, and who knows but that at one time he was a very important person."

"What makes you think it's a him anyway?" I enquired.

"Bone structure," she announced grandly. She lined herself up beside Gabriel to outline the contrast between male and female facial contours. At this point Gabriel decided that he had more pressing things to attend to and removed himself from the discussion. He always found Frances's mental dexterity slightly confusing. She had the ability to carry on three conversations at the one time: the conclusion of the conversation she had had with the person she had met before you, the relevant conversation of the moment, and the one she was carrying on inside in her own head. You had to find your way between the three lines of thought and pick out what applied to the subject on hand.

"What will we call him?" I asked.

"Hitler," Frances announced.

"Why Hitler?"

"He came from Germany and he is after causing a disturbance," she declared.

"But he is not German," I protested. "He only went for a visit."

"True," Frances admitted, "and as well as that he did not have much choice in the matter."

"All the more reason why he should not be called Hitler," I asserted.

"Well, what about Churchill?" she asked. "Didn't he have some connection with Innishannon?"

"He only came here on holidays; he's not buried here," I protested. "But why can't we just call him an ordinary name? He was probably a very ordinary fellow called Jack or something."

"Jack in the box! Perfect!" Frances declared.

"Well, I had not quite thought of him like that," I admitted.

"That's your problem," Frances proclaimed; "you don't think."

Before we got bogged down in a lengthy discussion on my mental limitations, I gave in gracefully. We called our visitor Jack, and that night he rested on our kitchen window in view of the old graveyard. He was almost back to base, but he still had a few detours to make.

The next morning when I awoke I looked out the

window at the old tower in the graveyard at the end of the village and thought about Jack. It seemed very casual to take him down and just replace him as if he had never been disturbed. After all, he was part of a body, and where you had a body you usually had a priest and doctor. As Jack's days of needing a doctor were long gone, we could dispense with that part of the ceremony, but maybe the presence of a clergyman was called for in the circumstances.

Now, our old graveyard is multi-denominational, for historical rather than ecumenical reasons, and gathered there are Catholic, Church of Ireland and various other bodies. As the devil you know is said to be better than the devil you don't, I decided to tackle the parish priest first. Tucking Jack under my arm in case I would need to produce evidence to establish the authenticity of my story and to prove that I was not suffering from hallucinations, I set out for the parish priest's house.

It was a lovely summer's morning, and as I walked up the hill I could well understand if Jack was glad to be back in Innishannon. Wherever he had been it could never have been as nice as his own place. I could almost sympathise with him for tripping up our correspondent, who had whipped him away without even as much as a by-your-leave. I was beginning to feel quite protective towards Jack. Frances had been right: a name had given him a whole new dimension. In some way I felt that he depended on me to see him safely home.

The parish priest did not quite see it like that. He sat by a blazing fire wearing three cardigans, and looked at me as if I had landed a dead cat at his feet. He was a very old man who felt the cold intensely, and the idea of exploring a dark, damp tomb did not appeal to him. I could understand his reluctance but at the same time I had Jack's future to think about.

"My child," he said in a wheezing voice, "that graveyard is no longer under our jurisdiction."

"But, Father," I protested, "it could have been when he was first buried there."

"I have no way of knowing that," he said decisively, and that was the end of the road for Jack and myself as far as he was concerned. As I walked out the avenue, I found myself humming the air of "O'Brien has nowhere to go".

Next, with Jack still under my arm, I decided to pay a house call to the Church of Ireland minister, who lived at the other end of the village. He was a chubby little man with a beaming smile which faded gradually as I told my story.

"Unbelievable!" he declared.

I pulled Jack out from under my arm and proceeded to unwrap him to prove how believable it was.

"Put it away!" he said, holding up a shielding hand, and I began to wonder about all these men who were supposed to look after the dead.

"Well, now," he said, "this is the position. That

graveyard is County Council property and no longer our responsibility."

It seemed to me that the churches were of the opinion that burial, like birth, could only happen once. When you are buried, that's the end of the road as far as they are concerned. If you make a bit of a come-back after that, then that's not their problem. As we walked down the road, I wondered where Jack and myself would go from here. One tale that I had never forgotten since my schooldays was the story of the Little Red Hen, which ended with the line: "I'll do it myself, said the little red hen."

I decided I would perform the obsequies myself.

When I got home I rang Frances.

"We are going to bury Jack," I told her.

"Who is going to do it?" she asked.

"You and I," I said.

"Proper order," she declared; "he could not be in better hands."

"You can read the directions and I'll do the burying."

"Sounds like a kind of a DIY job," she said.

"Exactly," I agreed. "After all, Jack came to us, so we'll finish the journey with him."

"When will we do it?" she asked.

"This evening around eight o'clock; I'll call for you," I told her.

"Don't forget to bring Jack," she said.

That evening as we approached the gate of the old graveyard, it started to rain.

"Maybe we should cancel the funeral," Frances suggested.

"No way!" I declared. "You don't cancel funerals because of the rain."

"That's because the chief mourners would object, and we don't have that problem," she suggested.

"Maybe they are here in spirit," I said, "so let's get started. You begin reading out the directions."

Frances peered down at the barely legible writing.

"I forgot my glasses," she announced. "We'll have to postpone it."

"Did you ever hear of a funeral postponed because the undertaker forgot his glasses?" I demanded.

"This is no ordinary funeral," she protested.

"Give me that piece of paper," I instructed and I tried to make out the writing.

"My God, he is a dreadful writer," I complained.

"All doctors write like that," Frances pronounced wisely; "something to do with the mystique of medicine."

"It says so many footsteps in from the gate," I said, measuring it in long strides.

"Does that mean men's or women's strides?" Frances asked.

"Men's, I presume, seeing as how he was a man," I answered.

"You can never presume in these cases," Frances informed me.

She was soon proved right because when I came to the next instruction which said turn left it meant walking through a stone wall. Something had gone wrong somewhere.

"Give me the instructions," Frances demanded.

"But I thought that you couldn't see without your glasses," I said.

"Well, maybe I'm still better than you," she told me. "So let's go back to the gate again."

At this point Jack's paper coffin was beginning to disintegrate in the rain and I was afraid that he would come out to meet us before we were quite ready for him. So back to the gate we went again and, with Frances calling out directions, I proceeded into the graveyard slowly. We had a few false stops and starts and Frances announced, "The fool that wrote this had no sense of direction."

Finally we arrived at the door of a big stone tomb with a rusty iron door.

"Well, this is it. Home, sweet home," Frances declared, but I wanted to make doubly sure.

"Will we go back to the gate again and follow the directions so as to be quite certain?" I asked.

"Oh, you of little faith!" Frances protested.

We went back to the gate again and while Frances carried Jack I called out the instructions and to my surprise we arrived back at the same tomb door.

"Now we are sure," Frances declared, handing Jack over to me.

"He's all yours now," she told me.

"Well, the first thing now is to open this door, so hold Jack a minute until I see if it's possible," I said, handing Jack back to her. I pulled back the rusty bolt, which moved with a squeaky protest, and the door swung back slowly. Inside it was pitch dark.

"We should have brought a flashlamp," I moaned.

I peered into the tomb and discerned steps leading down just inside the door.

"Give me Jack," I said. Putting my foot out slowly, I proceeded cautiously down the steps. As my eyes grew accustomed to the darkness, I began to be able to see fairly clearly from the light coming in through the door. The tomb was square, damp and quite small; questionable bits and pieces littered the floor. In the corner stood a very old coffin and this I knew straight away was where Jack had been lifted from. The question now was whether I had the courage to put him back in. If I left him there on the floor, I would feel I had not quite finished the job that had been entrusted to me. Slowly I approached the coffin and put my hand out to see if the lid would lift easily. It did. I eased it up gingerly, just high enough for Jack to fit through, and then I closed my eyes so that I could not see what was inside. Gently I put Jack back into his resting place and let the lid down slowly.

"What are you doing in there?" Frances called nervously.

I gave a last look around the tomb before coming briskly up the steps.

"God, I'm glad that's over!" I said.

We pushed in the heavy iron door and shot the rusty bolt.

"I'm sure that he is in the right place," I said positively.

"We can't be sure of that until the day of general judgement," Frances pronounced ponderously. "If a guy comes out of here with two heads and another with no head at all, then you have made a mistake. If they are all intact, then the job was oxo!"

That night I wrote to the worried medical student. I never again heard from him and I hope that he never again heard from Jack.

HOLY BUNS

THE ST JOSEPH'S Young Priest Society were in Knock that day. I stood and watched the procession pour out of the basilica. Wave after wave of people carrying banners representing parishes from all over Ireland. They were like a mountain stream that came on and on. Men with office faces, factory faces, drivers' faces and men with farm faces. Women with designer clothes, boutique clothes and chain store clothes. People from different ends of the parish social ladder and off all the rungs up along as well. As I watched them the thought came into my mind that these people were as constant as the Northern star and as indestructible in their ways as the Mayo rocks around them. Then came the bishops, priests and altar boys in white surplices. They frothed out of the basilica like milk out of a bucket. I looked well at the nuns in their religious habits, observing closely an endangered species.

All these people blended together in a sea of technicolour religion, while thirsty children in their best clothes swung off praying mothers, as they demanded crisps and minerals. This was the public face of Knock. For many of them it was an annual pilgrimage and one of their summer outings. The car parks were lined with buses that had left country parishes all over Ireland before the dawn had broken. Driving along the quiet early morning roads they had said fifteen decades of the rosary and sung hymns to Our Lady.

It is devotion to Our Lady that draws them all here, because this more than anywhere else in Ireland is her place. She appeared here on the gable end of the church with St John and St Joseph in 1879, and since then the people of rural Ireland have made this their place of pilgrimage to her. She is "at home" to them here because this barren corner of Mayo is like many country parishes and poorer than a lot of them. The Queen of Heaven who would visit here is approachable rather than regal. They tell a story in Knock that Monsignor Horan rang up heaven to ask God to open his airport, and when God refused, he was asked to send his mother. God said, "She'll be delighted to come, because she was never there before." But they know in Knock that God was only codding!

They tell another story about a local beggar woman who, shortly after the apparition had taken place, called to the parish priest who was always very generous to her. The following day she called to his not-so-generous brother who was parish priest in the next parish, but he turned her from the door empty handed. As she left she shouted back at him from the garden gate, "No wonder Our Lady never appeared on your gable end!"

The atmosphere at Knock on that sunny summer's day was a mixture of a parish carnival and a country station. The children obviously came for the day out and had a great time buying holy bric-a-brac in the various shops which satisfied all kinds of religious fervour. Many of the adults, however, performed their pilgrimage duties with great attention to detail: having made the Stations of the Cross, they then said the fifteen decades of the rosary around the church, some silently and others in groups.

Some of the people who came were in the need of extra comfort and they lined up for the blessing of the sick – people for whom wheelchairs, crutches and walking aids are part of their way of life. They came not for miracle cures, but for spiritual strength and stamina; and because they find it here, they come back again and again. Broken people find God because they need him.

I went into the then empty basilica and looked around this huge stadium that Monsignor Horan built to shelter his visiting flock. As I sat there a family came in. In a wheelchair sat a waxen-faced, hunch-backed, middle-aged lady whose wasted legs dangled on to the support at the front of the chair. Her faded blonde hair was wound around her head in an old-fashioned braid and it framed her shrunken face like a halo. She was pushed along by an overweight sister who wore a blue crimplene dress that was too short and too tight. Wisps of grey hair framed a red face that had never seen the inside of a beauty parlour. She was a bigger and healthier copy of her sister. Her husband, a pot-bellied, balding man with braces, led a beautiful wide-eyed little boy by the hand. The child embodied the finer points of the adults and was probably the miraculous product of a late marriage. There was about them a harmony of movement, as if they were moulded together by the same thought process. They came to the front of the altar, where a satin-robed Our Lady with outstretched hands smiled down on them. Around her feet were bunches of many-coloured roses that cascaded on to the floor. The family gathered in a semi-circle around the statue and stood wordlessly looking up at her. This was the reason for their visit. Then the mother reached forward, picked a rose and handed it to the lady in the wheelchair. She took it with her twisted fingers and smiled wistfully at the rose while the others looked on. No words were spoken but the three of them were like a bodyguard around her, and then the little boy reached up and touched her face with his small brown fingers. It was an expression of gentle love. As they left the basilica there was no sound but the swish of the wheelchair. They were a solid unit with a calm unquestioning acceptance of their wheelchair burden. This was the private face of Knock. It is for such as these, the unso-phisticated and often very courageous people, who sometimes struggle silently under heavy burdens and fight isolated battles against poverty and emigration, that Knock provides a corner of spiritual sustenance.

Later that evening another face of Knock emerged as I watched a middle-aged, well-married couple walk slowly outside around the old chapel saying the rosary. The swaying beads knocked off their knees as she gave out the decades and he answered. They walked slowly, completely intent on their mission, with no children to hinder their concentration. The children had probably been farmed out to the neighbours for the day or else were busy stuffing themselves in one of the many shops. But there could be no doubt but that there were children somewhere, as the couple had that battered look that can only be derived from rearing children on a limited income. She wore a good suit that had been fashionable a few years earlier and was now revived by a new blouse and her shoes that had seen her through a few summers still looked good because she was the kind of woman who would look after her clothes well. The husband was an example of her good housekeeping, well scrubbed and washed to within an inch of his life. He had the appearance of a solid, easy-going, hard-working man, satisfied with his lot, including his well-meaning, managing wife. Theirs could have been a journey of thanksgiving or petition, but whatever way the wind was blowing they were giving it their all. This was the ordinary face of Knock.

It is the holy water women who give Knock its

colour. They rattle off their prayers to Our Lady because she is as familiar to them as one of their neighbours, they are in such regular communication with her. They fill up countless plastic bottles with holy water which they take home to bless their parishes. Theirs is an unanalysed and unquestioning faith. They are on their way to heaven and shall not be moved, and they are the real face of Knock.

In the tea shops of Knock, tables covered in bright gingham cloths were laden with large plates overflowing with iced buns of many colours. Comfortable women and slim teenagers poured tea out of giant teapots to wash down the pink, lemon and white iced buns. I think of these as the holy buns of Knock, which provide the strength for further prayer. Here parents and children were united over cups of tea and glasses of Coke while Knock pencils and rosary rings were examined. Neighbouring women who had travelled on the same bus took advantage of the opportunity to discuss parish affairs. They had travelled and prayed together and now it was time for a chat, but as the queue of people waiting for tea and buns got longer, they were gently edged towards the door.

They went to confession and got mass cards signed and after a final visit to the church streamed back to the car parks. Missing children were rounded up, and a man who had come along because some well-meaning woman had talked him into it had to be run to ground in a quiet pub. As the buses headed

homewards the rosary was said and then the singers on the bus entertained their fellow passengers.
At the half-way mark on the homeward journey the
bus pulled into a hotel for a pre-arranged meal,
and when the second leg of the journey began sleep
caught up with many of the pilgrims. They dozed off
to the sound of "Hail Queen of Heaven" and woke
up miles down the road in the midst of "The Fields
of Athenry".

When they arrived home in the early hours of the
morning, into quiet country towns and villages, cars
were waiting to collect them; sleeping children were
transferred like rag dolls on to back seats. The long
day was over, but next year they would come again.

MAURICE

Long, lean body
supported and borne
on rigid iron sticks.
You have within
a glowing spirituality
which overflows like lava,
blinding us to your limitations
and infusing warm richness
into us who are without
your buried fire.

THE WEDDING GARMENTS

MARY MY SISTER's voice on the phone was hesitant, which immediately made me suspicious.

"What are you doing on Saturday?" she asked tentatively.

I wondered what she was up to. Might I finish up the following Saturday painting a neighbour's ceiling or travelling miles to an auction? Either was a possibility where my sister was concerned, but neither case would have caused the present uncertainty in her voice. A red alert went on in the back of my mind as I wondered what on earth I was letting myself in for.

Cautiously I said, "Nothing in particular. What had you in mind?"

"It's the wedding," she said.

For weeks we had talked about nothing else but the forthcoming wedding of her daughter. It was the first family nuptials of our collective children, and I had already discovered that there is nothing like a wedding to muster the family troops, or at least the female regiments. "Us aunts", who had during turbulent teenage years been relegated to the back benches of unconsulted opinion, had all of a sudden been dragged out of the cupboard of family skeletons for our views on wedding etiquette to be gravely consulted by young adults.

We were at this stage all suitably attired to maintain family self-respect and to impress the prospective in-laws. The fact that the groom's family was from the other end of the country and knew very little about us instilled the feeling that we were on parade and a guard of honour was called for around the bride.

Soon we thought we had covered every contingency as far as family appearances were concerned. A few great-aunts had been coaxed out from under layers of winter woollies to don slim-fitting suits. Aunt Maud had declared that double pneumonia was the price to be paid for this act of lunacy. She told her cap-wearing husband Uncle Tom that if she was prepared to risk death for the family honour then he would have to do his bit as well. He was instructed that he was to keep his cap off and his mouth shut and stand up and sit down when he was told for the entire day of the wedding. He complained that without his cap he could finish up with frost-bite in the head. Aunt Maud assured him that it was unheard of in the field of medical science, and that she was far more likely to suffer a freezing end. Uncle Tom told her that all she had to do in her case was to don a warm knickers but that that choice was not open to him. It was his other extremity that was under threat. Because I had never seen Uncle Tom without his cap, which he wore even in bed, I decided that I might not know him without it. The new in-laws were not going to recognise the real us. In fact we might not even recognise ourselves on the day!

With all these outlying difficulties duly considered and solved, what could be worrying my sister just a week before the wedding?

"What's the problem?" I asked, hoping that after all the family upheaval the whole damned thing was not to be called off.

"It's Susan," she groaned. A deep sigh swished into my ear at even the mention of her youngest daughter, who at fourteen was proving that the generation gap was alive and kicking.

"What about Susan?" I enquired tactfully.

"She went shopping for her outfit yesterday," my sister announced.

"Well, that's a step in the right direction anyway," I said, because Susan had refused to go shopping when the other sisters had done theirs weeks previously.

"You should see what she arrived home with," my sister moaned.

"Oh, not suitable?" I asked sympathetically.

"Suitable!" she said dramatically. "It looks like something that came in a parcel from America about thirty years ago. After all the effort the grandaunts have made! If they see her in this gear, they'll have a collective stroke."

I had never heard of a collective stroke, but that

did not put it outside the realms of possibility. This wedding was pioneering new complaints for medical science.

"What's to be done?" I asked, feeling that it was my job to be supportive. After all, as the Jacob's lady used to say, it could be my problem some day.

"Will you take her shopping next Saturday?" she implored, sounding as if she was asking me to leave home and sail single-handed around the world.

"No problem," I assured her, feeling as confident as the man who had coined the phrase.

"Oh, thank God," she gasped. "That's a weight off my mind. If she and I go together at this stage, we might end up not talking for the wedding. I couldn't take that chance!"

Then, maybe because she felt that I should be prepared in some way, she asked, "Have you any idea what you are letting yourself in for?"

"Well," I said, "I have gone shopping with the boys and that was not too bad."

"Ah," she said wisely, "there is no comparison. Boys are a walk-over. Girls are a whole different kettle of fish. But," she continued as if to ease her guilt, "it will be an education to prepare you for the future."

Early the following Saturday morning, Susan and I met outside Roches Stores. Her straight blonde hair formed two long curtains on either side of her small oval face and her fringe almost hid her eyes from view. Her slight figure was buried in a baggy jacket reaching her knees, beneath which bleached denims sported a well-worn look and Doc Marten boots finished the dishevelled appearance.

"Will we start here?" I asked diplomatically, having decided before leaving home that under no circumstances was I going to get embroiled in an argument.

"No way!" Susan said firmly.

"Where to, so?" I asked demurely; she cocked a suspicious eye in my direction.

"Follow me," she instructed and strode ahead with her hair and her jacket flying behind her. I ran to get abreast of her, taking care at the same time not to get my toes pulverised by the Doc Martens.

She led me down narrow side-streets and around sharp corners and then suddenly disappeared into a black doorway. When I dived in after her, I nearly took a nosedive down steps inside the door. Luckily I recovered my balance before hitting the floor. The assistant inside rolled her eyes to heaven and her expression told me that they did not normally number staggering geriatrics among their clientele. As I recovered my bearings, my ear-drums were assaulted by pounding music which started a headache at the base of my skull. The lighting was for some strange reason black and green, and I wondered how anyone could succeed in buying anything in this hell-hole.

Susan had no such problem and was busy whipping dresses off the rack and holding them up for viewing. The entire colour range seemed to consist of black, brown, navy and sludge green, and I thought that they would be well suited to the business of dressing chief mourners.

"I'll try this on," Susan announced, swinging a plum-coloured model in my general direction, and disappeared behind a purple curtain. She appeared shortly afterwards looking like a washed-out version of a Raggedy Anne doll. I understood then what my sister had meant when she had talked of the dress that had come in a parcel from America thirty years ago. The trouble with this particular little number was that it would probably never have been posted in the first place. I shook my head because verbal communication was out of the question. Susan promptly disappeared with a black beaded dress and returned, a miniature scarecrow. If she had sat on the ditch of her grandfather's potato field in her black satanic outfit, no crow would have ventured within flying distance of her. If we brought it home, her mother would have me locked up.

"Let's try around," I shouted.

"I can't hear you," she shouted back, so I went to the door and waved goodbye to demonstrate my intentions. The assistant's expression told me forcefully that interfering mothers and aunts should be put down.

Having made my escape, I leaned against the wall outside to accustom my eyes to normal lighting and to recover my equilibrium. A woman passing by seemed to have difficulty in making up her mind if

I was drunk or in need of medical attention. With a concerned frown she continued on her way.

When Susan joined me she grinned triumphantly and said: "Not your scene."

"No, Susan," I admitted, "definitely not my scene, but let's give my scene a try."

We went into one of the large chain stores and took the elevator to the quiet realms of the fashion floor where lighting was normal and at least we could see what we were buying. This, I thought, was more like it, but my opinion was not shared by my shopping companion. As I searched through rows of brightly coloured teenage rails, she stood watching me with a bored look on her face and chewed her nails. She had suddenly switched off and decided that dressing her was my problem and had nothing to do with her. Finally, after my offering about ten garments for her consideration, which were all received with a shrug of the shoulders and a shake of the head, I suggested that she should try one on, just to see how it looked. She shrugged her shoulders again and the pronounced look on her face became even more sullen as she said with a sigh, "If it keeps you happy."

I went with her to the door of the fitting room and it swung open to reveal rows of semi-nude females struggling in and out of different garments. She stopped dead, like a show jumper faced with an insurmountable wall, and turned on me with blazing eyes.

"If you think," she said dramatically, stopping for effect after each word, "that I am going to take my clothes off in the middle of all those old biddies, you have something else coming to you."

"Oh," I said, not sure how to handle this development.

Suddenly and to my surprise she leaned forward and whispered conspiratorially into my ear, "I want to buy a bra."

"The lingerie department is just here," I said, thinking this might give us breathing space. "Let's look at them."

"You," she told me in a fierce whisper and again stopping for effect after every word, "are going to buy it, and while you are at it, don't talk to me!"

"Oh," I said for the second time within minutes. Words were failing me. Nevertheless, I proceeded to pick out a little bra which I duly presented to an assistant, who probably wondered how I had lived so long and developed so little. I then went in search of Susan and found her hiding behind the swimsuits.

"Now panties," she hissed at me.

This time I did not need to be instructed and went to inspect the different models, but because I thought that she might like to decide on colour, I brought a brief pink one back to behind the swim-suits for inspection.

"Only floozies wear those!" she spat at me, rolling her eyes to heaven.

Then I became aware that someone was watching

us and I turned around to be met by the appraising gaze of the security man.

I quickly returned the pink panties, picked up some white ones and went straight to the till without checking back with my control tower, suspecting that the security man had decided that behind the swim-suits was where we were stockpiling the loot.

When I returned I found that she had selected a black bikini that was briefer than brief. That she intended to parade around in this, which was one step from nudity, after refusing to undress in a fit-ting room defied logic. But at this stage I was fol-lowing blind instinct not logic. Back I went to the till under the watchful gaze of the assistant and the security man.

It was my first experience of what it felt like to be at the wrong side of the law and I decided that my future did not lie in that direction. A break was needed.

"Let's have lunch," I suggested.

"Oh, great," she declared.

At least we were of one mind in something, I thought.

"Let's go to MacDonalds," she suggested brightly, all signs of sullenness melting like dew in the morn-ing sun.

"I'd prefer somewhere a bit quieter," I said plaintively.

"Right," she said, "let's split and meet up again afterwards."

It was a great idea as we were in dire need of a rest from each other. I retreated to a quiet restaurant where I eased off my shoes under the table, closed my eyes and reviewed the situation. Half the day was gone and all we had to show for our time was a bra which might not even fit, three pairs of white panties and a black bikini. Scarcely what was needed for a wedding outfit. The family honour was riding on my back and time was closing in on me. Nevertheless I decided to put the problem on hold to effect a recovery and enjoy my lunch, to which I added a glass of wine to mellow me into a more relaxed frame of mind. A friend who happened to be in the same restaurant stopped at my table and I told her about my mission.

"Ah," she said glancing at the glass of wine, "you need more than that. On a day like this a bottle of whiskey would not go amiss."

She was the mother of four teenage daughters, so I knew that it was the voice of experience speaking.

After lunch we set forth again. At first I was very positive, relaxed by the rest and the wine. I felt sure that it was only a matter of time before we hit on the right outfit, but as the afternoon wore on so did my positive thinking evaporate. Susan walked past rows of what I considered suitable clothes and refused to look at them. When I hopefully dangled one outfit before her, she almost fainted with horror and rolled her eyes so high that they disappeared up under her fringe. She demanded to know if I was trying to turn her into a bog-woman. I restrained myself from telling her that our bogs were one of our great assets, and that a bog-woman was someone to be treasured. She fitted on a few outfits just to keep me quiet, but she stared at herself in the mirror with such a look of resigned suffering on her face that I accepted that we were going nowhere. In one shop she picked up a vile green miniskirt that her grandfather would have declared was "just below the water-line", and it took all my diplomacy to part her from it without a stand-up fight.

We were within half an hour of closing time and no wedding garment in sight! I was looking into the face of defeat and Susan and I were barely on speaking terms when suddenly I saw it. There it was at the end of the rail, a little blue suit that I knew straight away could be dead right. I grabbed it and ordered Susan in my best sergeant-major's voice: "Follow me!"

We ran into the fitting room and because time was of the essence now there was no time for Susan to worry about the semi-clad females around her. What had been a morning problem was now no problem at all. She whipped off her jacket, enormous sweater and jeans and jumped out of her Docs. On went the well-cut blue miniskirt that rested easily on her slender hips and flattered her long slim legs. She slipped on the little jacket and it fitted like a dream. My eyes met hers in the mirror and her face lit up with delight. The duckling had turned into a swan.

"It's beautiful," she gasped.

"You're beautiful," I told her, and we threw our arms around each other and did a victory dance up and down the fitting-room, much to the amusement of the other occupants.

We had been snatched from the jaws of defeat by the little blue suit. I cringed a little when I saw the price tag, but it did not deter me; even if we had to have a church-gate collection it was worth it. Susan, however, was at an idealistic age and thought that you could get a whole outfit in a second-hand shop for a fiver, so I hid the price-tag from her and hurried out to the till while she was dressing.

She caught up with me in the queue, and when the assistant rang up the amount, she squealed in horror.

"Put it back!" she screamed. "I can't wear that much money on my back and half the world starving!"

"If we buy this we'll keep the people who made it from starving," I snapped at her.

"At least put half of it back," she implored. "We'll just take the jacket because they are separates anyway."

"You can't go to the wedding in just a jacket," I told her, whipping the bag off the counter. We were now surrounded by a little gathering of sympathetic-looking women. It was difficult to know where their sympathies lay, and I did not care. I strode towards the door, and now it was Susan's turn to run after me. Suddenly she caught up with me and slipped her small hand into mine.

"Sorry," she said, "it's a lovely suit but I don't think that I deserve it."

"Would you like to earn it?" I demanded.

"How?" she asked.

"For the next week be as helpful as you can at home and keep your opinions to yourself," I told her.

"You sound like Aunt Maud," she said.

"Is it a bargain?" I asked.

"It's a bargain," she agreed.

That night her mother came on the phone and, after expressing her delight at Susan's outfit, she asked, "What did you do to Susan?"

"Why?" I questioned.

"She's suddenly angelic for some reason," I was told.

"Blackmail," I informed her.

"I don't care what it is," she sighed blissfully, "as long as it works."

I discovered that my success carried another, unexpected price-tag when after a few minutes' conversation she said casually, "Aunt Maud was wondering if you would take Uncle Tom shopping for a new cap and suit."

"But," I protested, "isn't Uncle Tom going to wear his navy suit that he got for the IFA dinner a few years ago?"

"Well, that was the case, but you know the vagario that Aunty Maud has about his cap. Well, he's refusing to take it off and she's insisting that he buy a new one. Then she thinks that a new cap will show up how old the suit is and so now she wants him to get a new suit as well. He's stone mad over it and will only buy it if she stays at home and lets him off on his own."

"But he won't be on his own if I'm with him," I said.

"Uncle Tom won't mind you, and Aunty Maud thinks that you are better than nothing," she informed me.

The following Monday, Uncle Tom and I met up at lunch-time. It had to be that late in the day because he was of the opinion that it was uncivilised to go shopping any earlier.

"Let's have a bite to eat before we start," he suggested.

"Have we time?" I asked.

"All the time in the world, girlie," he told me. "Let's go to a decent hotel where we can sit down in comfort. I'm too old now to be running around gathering up bits and pieces on a tray."

His idea of shopping and mine were poles apart but his had a lot to recommend it. We sat down to a beautiful meal in the well-insulated quietness of a comfortable hotel. Afterwards he pulled out his pipe in the lounge and puffed away contentedly. As the hands of the clock wound onwards I ventured: "How long will your shopping take?"

"Yerra, about half an hour," he told me.

"But they might not have what you want in the first shop," I suggested.

"Why not?" he asked mildly.

"Well, different shops keep different types of suits," I said foolishly.

"We're not going to different shops," he told me.

"Oh," I said.

"Anyway," he decided, rising to his feet, "we might as well get a move on. There's no more to be done here." We walked down the street and around a corner. He stood back in front of a shop that I had never noticed before. "In here now," he said.

The little shop had a solid oak door and window and the lettering above them boasted the craftsmanship of earlier days. The window was tastefully dressed with an incredible variety of menswear, clearly the work of a person with an eye for perfect colour co-ordination. We went into the small shop which consisted of a short timber counter on our right, behind which rows of shelves reached from ceiling to floor and were packed with shirts; on our left the same again, laden with sweaters. Not a suit in sight.

At the end of the short counter, narrow timber stairs curved steeply upwards, and just then a pair of legs appeared behind the timber bannisters. They descended and a short, stocky, middle-aged man came into view. Dressed in matching fine tweeds with a measuring tape around his neck, he was sandy-haired and ruddy-faced, and he broke into a delighted smile when he saw Uncle Tom.

"Well, how are you?" he said. "The old navy number must be calling it a day."

Uncle Tom did not have the navy suit on him and it impressed me that he remembered, but Uncle Tom took it for granted.

"This is my niece," Uncle Tom told him.

"The bodyguard," he smiled and, rubbing his hands together, enquired, "what's the occasion?"

"A family wedding," Uncle Tom told him.

"Couldn't be better," he responded and, sweeping his arm in a grand gesture towards the stairs as if we were ministers of state, he invited us to "come this way".

We emerged on to another floor, a duplicate of the ground one, but here rows of suits hung in military precision and yet another flight of stairs curved upwards.

"Sit down here," he invited Uncle Tom, indicating a large, comfortable leather armchair of a kind which I associated with select men-only clubs. "And for you, my dear," he smiled, producing a padded footstool.

"Now," he said, clapping his hands together, "let's get started."

There was no doubt but that he knew his business inside out and delighted in it.

"No change in measurements I'd say," he observed. "But just in case..." and he whipped the measuring tape so fast around Uncle Tom's ample proportions that I marvelled that he had time to take in the details.

"Just as I thought," he said, "you're keeping fit."

"Now, let's see," he said to himself, and I felt that this was an artist at work. He walked along the rails, mentally eliminated unsuitable models and then nodded his head in approval when something pleased his fastidious eye. He swung off the suit that found favour and laid it across the back of a chair beside Uncle Tom, where he could be getting accustomed to the feel of the material. On his walk around he picked up just three suits, but I knew somehow that any one of them would be right. Then he lifted down two huge fashion books and placed them in front of me.

"These are this year's styles," he told me.

He was about to launch into the newest fashion details when Uncle Tom declared: "Whist up, man, and don't be confusing us. That girl knows as little about men's fashions as I do."

He smiled tolerantly at our admission of ignorance.

"Now then," he said, "which of these would you prefer?"

"This one," Uncle Tom decided, pointing at a navy one, which I thought was rather a pity as it was almost a duplicate of the one hanging up at home in the wardrobe.

"Good choice," our man declared, and I felt disappointed in him, but he soon recovered his ground without blinking an eyelid.

"This one, however," he continued, "is of a slightly better quality." And he picked up a dark grey suit that was the essence of respectability.

"Slip on the jacket now and if we're on the right track we'll try the pants."

Uncle Tom eased himself out of the deep chair where he had been reclining in regal fashion. The jacket fitted like a glove and gave him the appearance of an elderly statesman.

"Slip on the pants now," he was invited, and while he withdrew to the fitting room to do so, our man disappeared down the stairs. He came back up laden with shirts, ties and caps. When Uncle Tom reappeared, he looked splendid. When it was decided to their mutual satisfaction that it had everything that was needed in a suit, the next step was the shirt. Our man knew exactly what was required and gently guided Uncle Tom in the right direction, and likewise with the tie. It was all done with the utmost diplomacy and skill, and the end result was a perfectly tailored country gentleman.

So far there had been no mention of the cap and I would have thought that he had forgotten it had I not known that a bundle of them were lurking in a corner outside of Uncle Tom's vision. Parting Uncle Tom from his cap was a bit like unveiling the chalice, for it covered his holy of holies.

Without batting an eyelid our man brought forward three caps for review: "They are still making them, thank God," he said. "When this crowd go out of business, it will be a sad day for the cap wearer."

Uncle Tom examined the caps in great detail, and I realised that this required a far weightier decision than choosing the rest of the outfit. After a long and intensive examination, one found special favour with him.

"That's a grand cap," he finally declared, and slipped off his old one. With the removal of his per-petual cap, Uncle Tom's white bald dome came into view. He looked exposed and vulnerable. Bald heads that are continually open to the weather become hardened off like greenhouse flowers put out in the garden. But those constantly covered become deli-cate and their coming out is akin to the exposure of the female bosom. Uncle Tom eased on his new cap gingerly and gently rocked it up and down so that it would mould itself around the contours of his head. Satisfied, he smiled with relief. Our man smiled back in delighted agreement, and I sensed that he knew he had cleared the biggest hurdle.

"Shoes now," Uncle Tom demanded, sticking out a well-worn brogue, and within minutes the right shoes were on his feet.

"Might as well get an overcoat as I'm here," he decided, and our man disappeared up the spiral stairs to the floor above and arrived back with the perfect fit. Uncle Tom was newly dressed from head to toe, and all had been achieved with the minimum of fuss.

"That's it, so," he announced. "Bag the lot while

I'm togging off." And he disappeared into the dressing room.

On his return we proceeded down the stairs in a leisurely fashion and Uncle Tom asked, "What's the damage?"

When it was all added together, our diplomat knocked off a fiver for good luck and threw in a pair of matching socks; Uncle Tom paid up with a smile of appreciation on his face. As he handed over the money, he was asked, "Herself stayed at home?"

"She did indeed." And the unspoken thought between the two of them was clear: that it was the best place for her.

As we walked up the street, I looked at my watch. The whole thing had taken less than an hour.

"That's some shop," I said.

"The only place to buy anything," Uncle Tom told me.

The following Saturday at the wedding I watched Susan dance with a resplendent Uncle Tom, his suit and cap a perfect match. She looked lovely and I could see that she felt good in her blue suit as she caught my eye and winked.

A TIME TO GO

DRIFTING IN THAT semi-conscious state that exists between sleep and wakefulness, I soaked in the silence of the early morning. The bedroom door opened quietly and my husband came in; his calculated movements alerted my mind to the fact that something was wrong. He sat on the side of the bed, took my hand in his and said gently, "I have bad news." He hesitated, then continued: "Your father died last night."

"Oh, God," I protested. "I was going down to see him tomorrow. Oh, why didn't I go yesterday?"

Despite all the years that he had been with us, I felt cheated out of that one last visit, when perhaps I might have prepared my mind for the fact that it was to be the last time. There is never a right time to die.

Because he understood me so well, my husband left the room and quietly closed the door. I sat up in the bed and rested my chin on my knees and looked out through the window at the old tower at the end of the village. On that cold February morning, it was shrouded in an early morning mist. Scenes of childhood flitted through my mind. My father lighting the Christmas candle, his bald head shining in the candlelight. Coming into the yard late on a winter's evening with his two horses, their hooves and his heavy boots covered in the mud of the ploughed field. I remembered him turning the butter box that was his toolbox upside down on the kitchen floor and walking away when the job was done, leaving chaos behind him. The pride in his eyes when my mother was dressed up in her best suit and Sunday hat.

"Any of your daughters will never be as good looking as you, Len."

His impatience, which never seemed to annoy her because she was closer to him and understood him better than any of us. I remembered she had once told me that she wished to live longer than my father because she did not want to leave him on his own. She felt that no one could surround him with the love and patience that she alone could give him, and how right she was.

One of my young sons snuggled into the bed beside me and rubbed my face in sympathy.

"Don't be sad for Grandad," I said.

"Mom, it's you're crying, not me," he replied.

And sure enough, when I put up my hand, my face was wet with tears. I tucked him up in bed, dressed myself quickly and slipped down the stairs and out the side door. As I walked up the hill to the church, I felt a hard, unfamiliar lump and sadness within, and my mind seemed slightly out of focus. Our little church with its elegant steeple and mellow stonework stood welcoming in the grey of the morning. Inside, the altar candles flickered in the dim light. I entered the peace of the early morning weekday mass: no sermon and just a scattering of people. Our little church was a tranquil, soothing place where minds could drift and meditate.

As mass began I reached out and thought of my father, gone away beyond where human minds can stretch, and gently the peace of that holy place filled my heart. I should have gone around to the sacristy before the mass to tell Fr Seamus, who was a friend, to pray for my father during mass, but as yet my wound was too raw. I needed to heal a little before taking anyone else into my mind.

After breakfast we drove home through the early morning between trees and bushes huddled under grey frosty coats. When we came to a straight part of the road outside Macroom, I remembered one night a few years previously when I had been driving him home and we had got a puncture. We had both got out to size up the problem.

"Aren't I the useless devil?" he had said, "that I can't change a wheel. If it was a pony after losing a shoe, I'd be some help."

We had both laughed at his assessment of our dilemma, and just then a car with two men had come along and sorted us out in no time at all. He had been so grateful to them; he never took a kindness for granted and often spoke of those two men afterwards.

As we drove in the gateway leading down to our

house, I mentally pulled myself together to get a grip on myself so that I would not upset my mother. She was serene and calm, nothing to show her inner hurt but a face paler than usual and an extra-firm grip on my hand as we went into the parlour where my father was laid out in his best suit, his strong slender fingers interlaced across his chest. I was so glad that he was still there in his own place. His long, sensitive face was relaxed and peaceful in death; you could almost believe that he was asleep. Suddenly I found myself smiling and I could imagine him saying, "Aliceen, don't do Bessie Babe on it."

Bessie Babe was an old neighbour who loved crying at wakes and funerals and months afterwards could turn on the tears. My father had always maintained that she enjoyed crying.

"Well, Mom," I said, "we had better not do Bessie Babe on it."

"Yes," she smiled, "that would really annoy him."

Neighbours and relations came and went all day, and it was comforting to share memories of my father and the times that they had spent together. I knew him as a father; they knew him as a friend. Late in the afternoon I was sitting alone with him when an old man came into the parlour. He walked over to the coffin and, placing a hand on either side of it, looked down at my father. There was love and caring in his whole stance, and he reached out his hand and touched my father's face. He was saying goodbye. I sat motionless, not to disturb the farewell between two old friends. My mother came into the room and joined them and I felt that these three had known each other long before I was born. Afterwards I asked my mother about the old man, and she said simply, "They went to school together."

Later that evening the whole house filled up with people before the hearse came to take my father to the church. There is something profoundly touching about a removal from a family home where the owner has lived all his life. It was his final parting from his own place.

That night I stayed with my mother in their little flat where they now lived at the end of the family home. We slept in the bed that they had shared together for so many years and where he had died so quickly and peacefully the night before. It felt good to be so close to him. The fire that we had built up before going to bed sent long shadows across the low ceiling, and the room was filled with a quiet peace.

The following day after the funeral mass, we followed the hearse up the steep hill to the sprawling country graveyard. My father had never been a great attender at funerals and considered that to be my mother's department. If she did not go herself she dispatched one of us to represent the family and my father always advised cynically, "Make sure you are seen!"

He regarded a burial as a family affair whereas my mother considered it a neighbourhood affair. He had often laughed at her and said, "Len, the whole parish will turn up to bury you, but I'll have the place to myself."

He did not, however, have the place to himself, and I was surprised how comforted I felt by meeting so many of our old friends and neighbours. It is difficult to anticipate how one will react in any given situation until it actually happens. He was laid to rest in the old family grave under a limestone Celtic cross bearing his parents' names and those of many of his brothers and sisters. He was the last of that family and he joined his little son Connie, who had gone before him so many years before.

Friends and relatives who had travelled long distances came back to the house for a meal, and much talking was done. As the last of them drifted away, the early darkness of the February evening was drawing in. I put on a pair of wellingtons and wrapped myself in an old coat of my father's and walked down through the fields to the river that circled around the valley at the bottom of the farm. A light mist was falling and the wet grass squelched beneath my feet. Out there the quietness of the night was broken only by the water in the deep glaise as it tumbled over the stones. The fields were empty of animals and only the occasional rustle and scratching in the hedges reminded me that out there wildlife was always moving around in its own sheltered world. Reaching the river I sensed rather than saw its satin-black stillness and I thought how timeless is the flow of a river. For years my father had fished this river, and how he had loved it, but now he was gone from this place like seven generations of his family before him. Was there anything of him left around this river and these fields that he had walked so often? The scurrying clouds parted and a pale moon lit up the river bank, creating shadows in the dark water.

Silently my brother joined me and we stood together watching the water flow. He was the oldest and only brother and I was the youngest of his five sisters, and between us had always existed a special understanding. We walked along by the river talking as only people who are on the same mental wavelength can. As we walked I felt that the passing of my father was part of a natural pattern, and because his grandchildren were here to carry on, there was no cutting off. Part of him would always be here in his land.

Leaving the river, we followed an old path that I had not walked for many years. I remembered a very steep hill that we had trudged up every evening coming home from school. Now with the eyes of an adult, I looked at the gently sloping incline and laughed.

"My God," I said, "I used to think that this was a mountain and it's really only a little hill."

We walked up the gentle slope and turned our feet homewards.

Coming into my mother's flat, I found her sitting by the fire with the tea ready on a tray and toasting bread before the glowing fire.

"You went down to the river," she said, "just like your father. He always walked the fields to sort things out in his mind."

SPRING AND I

As I STOOD at the top of the stairs, the early morning sun peered in over my shoulder. It lit up the walls around me and highlighted the dust-laden cobwebs that draped from picture to picture. How long had they been there? During the long winter months, I had never noticed them. They had gathered in like a silent army all around the house.

If you are a collector of pictures or other useless articles that can be acquired at auctions, antique shops and craft fairs, then the price to be paid is the accumulation of numerous bits and pieces between which cobwebs can drape in comfort and on which dust can rest easily. If you then decide that they all have to be polished and kept in mint condition, they become a burden which takes all the joy out of your collection. My solution to the problem is to let them lie in comfort under their dusty jackets, which I delude myself gives them an air of shrouded antiquity. Occasionally, however, something happens to disturb my acceptance of their grey, restful mantles, and then a mental battle ensues. The sun had started two strains of thought. The lazy side of me said that I should leave things as they were while the more industrious side advised getting my act cleaned up to welcome in the spring.

That morning the cobwebs were not only draped between the pictures: they were also draped along my brain cells. Spring sunshine was sending its coded messages, but my brain was still too deeply anchored in winter to unscramble them. I turned my back on the cobwebs and decided to look in another direction. Behind me was a window through which the offending sun was probing its way with determination. It needed that determination because the grime on the window was trying bravely to prevent entry. The window, like my mind, was reluctant to let in the spring. Then the curtains caught my eye and their over-muted tones told the story of a long grey winter when smoke from an open fire had occasionally lost its sense of direction and curled seductively around them. While we had warmed our toes to the comforting heat, the smoke had been wrapping its silent arms around our curtains.

I walked around the house making a mental assessment of winter damage. It was a depressing experience. Energy was needed to turn back this grey tide of winter dust, but the only energy I could muster seemed to be possessed by my eyes, which were determined that I should not miss a mite of dust. So intense was my mood of inspection that I put on my glasses to enhance my vision. Short-sightedness had been my constant companion since childhood and sometimes it had proved to be a very desirable condition by eliminating unsightly views. That morning, however, I was not content to allow myself to shelter behind that comfort. But as I crawled around the house acting the martyr, a little voice of reason came to my rescue and coaxed me out into the garden.

Here the birds were singing and the cobwebs that draped across the shrubs glistened in the sunlight, proving that there is a place for everything. My mental cobwebs slowly drifted apart and a little light came into my mind. I examined the bare shrubs and found tiny buds just beginning to form. They looked delicate and vulnerable, not unlike my mental condition, and as I ran my fingers over their soft formation, I felt future flutterings within. The spring bulbs were bravely standing upright and their colour was in sharp contrast with the dark brown earth. A few weeks previously they had ventured up from their winter womb to bring a little colour into a garden suffering from the withdrawal symptoms of winter. Beside them the bridal wreath was cascading down over a stone bank, its snowy branches highlighted by the grass, bright after the rains of winter. The bees from the nearby hive were busy investigating this addition to their menu, a welcome variation after their long hibernation. During those cold months they had scarcely ventured beyond their front running board but now they were flying back and forth. They had got the message that spring was in the air.

As I watched their tireless pursuit of nectar, I began to feel slight pangs of guilt about my inertia.

The old garden seat looked very inviting, so I decided to sit in the sun just for a few minutes. Maybe if I sat still a reason for propelling myself into action might float into my brain. My garden is a place for thinking and relaxing and it has that appearance as well. The dogs were delighted and sat themselves down at my feet. The old one was content just to sit there, but the young fellow jumped up and down, slashing his long tail off my legs and whipping slobbering kisses across my face. He was full of the bounce of youth, but the old dog was content to lie and soak in the sun. I decided that I had a lot in common with the old dog. She believed in preserving her energy and only doing what was necessary. But suddenly, as the young fellow ran up the garden, she shot into action and tore after him. Even old bitches are not immune to spring fever.

As I sat in the sun, a solution to my problem presented itself. What I needed was to carry some of the garden life into the house to stimulate me into action. So I picked my first bunch of spring daffodils and arching branches of bridal wreath and carried them into the house. When they were arranged in a big jug in the centre of the kitchen table, they were like a crowd at a football match cheering me on, and they stimulated me into action.

Because the kitchen is the heart of the home, that was the place to begin. I opened the windows to let in the fresh air and I whipped off the curtains and thrust them into the washing machine. I danced along worktops like a drunken acrobat and lifted down pictures, while ancient spiders ran for shelter. Hot, soapy water ran down the walls, eradicating the stains made by an erratic deep fat fryer that was supposed to have a self-purifying system, but alas the walls told a different story. My collection of ancient jugs, which, like myself, has grown larger with the years, was immersed in the sink. I was up to my oxters in suds and loving every minute of it.

Buried inside in me is a charwoman who occasionally breaks out, and, when she does, nothing in the house is safe. The daffodils sat in the centre of all the chaos, willing me to bring everything to their bright and cheerful perfection. When it looked as if the kitchen might never again be restored to normality and I found it difficult to find a clear space to put a foot down, they stood there like an army of yellow cheerleaders. Flowers are beautiful but daffodils are special. They are the key that opens the door of spring, to tell us that it is time for a new beginning. When exhaustion threatened to overcome enthusiasm, they encouraged me to keep going, and gradually order was restored. The daffodils and the kitchen were at last in total harmony. Both were bright and beautiful, and I had taken the first step to welcome in the spring. I stood there feeling virtuous and at peace with the world.

The following days I moved around the rest of

the house like a white tornado and then out into the yard and garden. The spring enthusiasm of the bees had in some way communicated itself to me, and when my cleaning was complete, I went out into the garden to sit on the wobbly garden seat and watch them flying back and forth in a stream of activity. There is something very soothing about watching the bees as they go about their business with single-minded determination. With them there is no time for loitering, and if you put your ear to the back of their hive you will hear the hum of action within.

The birds showed a different approach to life, and in the ivy-clad wall behind the hives, they were busy getting their nests in order; unlike the bees, they took time off to sit on the branches of the nearby apple tree and sing with the sheer joy of living. Around the birds and bees the garden was waking up and rubbing the sleep of winter out of its eyes. The crucifixion of winter was behind, and they were getting ready for the resurrection. There was joy in the world of nature, and it awoke a responding chord in my heart. Even the old dog barked in delight as she chased the low-flying birds. She could never catch them and they both knew that, but spring is a time for flying a little higher than you thought possible and getting ready to dance with the sun on Easter Sunday morning.

WHITETHORN HONEY

Bridal hedges
Of whitethorn
Cascade on to
Summer meadows.
Under bulging wings
The gliding bees
Collect their virgin nectar,
Bearing it back
To humming hives.
Extraction time,
The pregnant combs
Release their ripened treasure,
Pouring golden liquid
Into sparkling jars.
In a deep cupboard
Spirit of warm days,
Bring to barren winter
The taste of whitethorn honey.

A Prayer and a Pint

Arriving in Ballybunion at one o'clock in the morning with rain lashing off the windscreen and flickering neon lights reflecting off the glistening street might not be everybody's idea of the right start to a holiday. But as I left the town behind and pulled up in front of the pink-washed house perched high over the sea, the holiday anticipation of childhood awakened within me.

Waves thundered against the black rocks below, shouting an awesome welcome, while sea spray like natural holy water showered me in a returning benediction. The one-walled castle silhouetted against the black angry sea presided over the restless monster at her feet with the ghostly eeriness of another life.

The following morning, after sleeping the sleep of the holiday-maker, I awoke to a howling wind which invited me out to do battle with it along the empty strand and up over the cliffs. The sea was at its most aggressive, belting off the grim, black, forbidding rocks that faced it with towering arrogance while the sea shot sprays of contemptuous spittle into its dark, brooding eyes.

Leaving turbulent nature behind, I arrived at the church where quietness was preserved inside the old grey stone walls, and candelabras of flickering candles penetrated the gloom. People slipped in quietly. Women with gentle faces and elastic stockings, the hallmark of childbearing years. Professional men with greying hair and soft leather shoes, their faces wearied from absorbing a daily barrage of other people's problems. Here they sat, relaxed in a temporary haven from their demanding world. Three priests came forth from the sacristy. It was to be a concelebrated mass, as holidaying priests swelled the presbytery staff: the first, a dark young man with the strutting arrogance of youth, the next a middle-aged one less assured, and finally an older man serene and confident that having come down a long road he was still going in the right direction.

Afterwards the people trooped out: the gentle women, the grey-haired men and others with tight, hard faces who had failed to find what they came for. Going into the paper shop across the road, I met the old priest coming out. We shook hands and chatted because we had known each other when he had been a young priest, I a brash teenager. We talked about the Ballybunion of my childhood, when people brought their own food and the guesthouse owners did the cooking. He told me how they had identified the different pieces of meat in the pots with bits of coloured ribbon. What gay pots bubbled on the Ballybunion cookers in those days!

Breakfast over, my energetic brood departed for the beach and I walked with my mother, now in the winter of her years, up into the town. The old on holidays are far less demanding than the young, as they have slowed down in the restful waters of old age and draw you into their tranquil pace for temporary respite. Other old people walked slowly along, shepherded by middle-aged sons or daughters, the role of former years reversed. Sometimes the shepherd was a jeans-clad, sneakered teenager, and granny and grandchild laughed happily together as he made fun of her infirmity, the young infusing the old with their reckless energy and carrying them along on their wave of high spirits.

My mother had a brooch in her bag that needed repair, so we set out for the jewellery shop at the far end of the town. Over the years she had brought stopped watches, alarm clocks and even bigger clocks on holidays to be repaired by an old man in this shop. He had been a wonderful watch and clock repairer and over the yearly holiday encounters had become a friend. He had died during the previous winter and now his son was in charge, so she was sailing in uncharted waters. When we arrived in the shop, she slowly opened her bag and took out a matchbox. The puzzled jeweller and I viewed the matchbox, but gradually the story unfolded as she eased it open to reveal an ancient brooch within.

Before the efficient young man could voice any disparagement about the article for repair, she told him serenely, "I bought this years ago from your father. He was a fine man and a splendid man for repairs. Built up his business that way, you know."

The young man was beaten before he started and he knew it. Examining the battered brooch with the faulty clasp, he promised to have it ready the following day.

Next on her agenda was a lady from home who had a pub in Ballybunion. When we called she was gone to the hairdresser, so we decided to have a drink in a quiet corner.

Around the pub were brown-legged yuppies in Bermuda shorts and fit-looking teenagers stretched across pool tables, displaying expanses of tanned backs above sea-blue denims. Sitting on a high stool in the corner of the counter in front of us was a man of indiscernible age with the assuredness of having been there when this pub had had a snug and before all the surrounding bodies had sailed in. This was his pub. A muddy-coloured gabardine overcoat with the look of many winters enveloped him and the high stool. A greasy cap which showed that it had been dried regularly beside a turf fire was pulled down firmly over his eyes and edged out over his black pint like a thatched roof. His nose was the only visible facial feature and it protruded between his pint and his cap like the beak of a giant crow. He sat ruminating on his stool, oblivious to these people who were not of his world.

Silently in beside him slipped a strange-looking

little man. My eyes had wandered around the pub and when they returned to the most interesting point, there the little man had appeared like a genie out of a bottle. He wore the coat of a suit belonging to a much bigger man, which reached almost to his knees, swinging over spindly legs encased in long grey socks pulled up outside his pants to his knees. The little man had enormous black boots laced half-way up his shin bones. His shrunken face had yellow, leathery skin stretched tautly across sharp bones, giving his eyes a prominent frog-like appearance. His crowning glory was a sparse crop of hair, so well oiled that little rivulets ran down his bony face like mountain streams between brown rocks.

A glamorous blonde barmaid approached him.

"My tay and bread and butter," he demanded.

She looked at him as if he had just crawled out from under a stone.

"He always gets it here," asserted the man from under the cap, with the implication in his voice that they had both been here before she was ever seen or heard of in this pub. Before she could decide on a course of action, a grey-haired man wearing the look of the owner came up along the bar. The little man relaxed visibly when he saw him.

"My tay and bread and butter, Boss?" he enquired.

"Of course, Jack," the boss assured him.

"Go over there," the man under the cap ordered, pointing to a corner seat and casting a contemptu-ous look at the pert barmaid. She was probably on holiday relief and he wanted to educate her as to who counted around here.

"She'll bring it over to you," he continued, making sure that she got the message.

The little man headed for the corner seat, his message bag slapping against his legs. I had not seen one of those bags for thirty years. Made of hard twine with a red band running around the middle, it had two strong cord handles. They had come out during the war and had been hung from the handlebars of bikes transporting household needs from country shops into the depths of rural Ireland. Very few could have survived this long, but here was one that, judging by the look of it, had served its owner well and developed a character of its own in the process. Years of rain, sunburn and miles of mud splashing on mountainy roads had given it a well-travelled, road-wise look. This little man and his message bag belonged together.

The problem solved, the man on the stool resumed his transcendental meditation. Suddenly, in the door came a man cycling without a bike. Almost as if the mechanism of his hip joints was faulty, he lifted his legs in a semi-circular movement high off the ground and they fell heavily by themselves. It was either that he had spent years cycling up against steep hills or that he lived in a very untidy house and automatically lifted his legs to get across miscellaneous pots and pans. Dressed in a dirty fawn suit, he had the face of a laughing gnome. He peered up at the man under the cap. They could only have come from the same hill. No salutations passed between them.

"Would you say that you're sixty-one?" was his opening remark.

"More," from under the cap.

"Sixty-two," he tried.

"More," came back from under the cap.

"Sixty-three?" in surprise.

"More," in the same tone.

"Sixty-four!" in disbelief.

"More," came back the toneless reply.

And so it continued until the fawn man said in amazement, "Sixty-nine!"

"Next spring," came the answer in a tone which implied that wonders would never cease.

That topic of conversation exhausted, from under the cap came the announcement, "Tom is taking the paper to court."

"Why?" asked the fawn man.

"They called him a jailbird."

"Well," with caution, "he was in jail."

"Only once, and once doesn't make him a jail-bird," came emphatically from under the cap.

That gave the fawn man something to think about, and having thought it over with a look of intense concentration on his face he finally pronounced, "Tom is in trouble with the paper, in trouble with the guards, in trouble with herself..." and with utter conviction he finished up, "Tomeen is in trouble with himself."

The man under the cap was not convinced. "The just man falls nine times," came the proclamation.

It is difficult to argue with a man who thinks bigger than God, so the fawn man knew that he had lost that round. His next shot was, "You'd be getting the dole all the time."

The man on the stool straightened up with the arrogance of movement that gave his rusty gabardine the air of a crimson cloak, and his burnt cap took on the splendour of a jewelled crown. The majesty of the Kerry hills was in his bearing as he spat out the words, "Never drew that in my life!" Stepping down from his high stool he had the dignity of a king descending from his throne and he swept out the door with the grandeur of a great actor taking his final curtain call.

I waited for the applause, but none came. Then I returned to reality and realised that this was not lunch-time theatre but real life, and I had been privileged to be present at a private viewing.

Later that morning my strong-willed seven-year-old bulldozed me unwillingly into a chilly navy-blue sea that splashed threateningly against my ankles of the same colour. In a navy-blue swimsuit I blended in perfectly with my surroundings. My daughter dived under scurrying waves and yelled at me to join her. As I high-stepped gingerly over the oncoming waves, I prayed that God might turn on a giant immersion somewhere out there in the Atlantic and take the murderous chill out of the freezing water. Having closed my eyes to add fervour to my prayer and to control my chattering teeth, I was taken unawares when a high-jumping wave swept over my head and showered me in its salty essence. Suddenly, as I came up gasping, the sun burst forth like a light in a darkening room and lit up the whole scene. The sea sparkled and white horses swept towards us wrapping us in their swirling tails. Looking out across the leaping waves that went on and on and reared higher and higher in the distance, I felt an overwhelming sense of exhilaration. Holding out my arms I felt part of a great creation and thanked heaven for the seven-year-old who had dragged me back into her sparkling world.

That afternoon the rain came down in sheets and turned the strand into a grey mist zone, and because I felt the need to be cosseted and by myself, I decided on a hot seaweed bath. The seaweed was collected from the Black Rocks when the tide was out and a bucketful thrown into the bath under a boiling hot water tap which burst the bubbles and drew the oil from the seaweed. The baths were attached to Mary Collins's tea rooms on the strand. She told me that in her younger days she boiled the seaweed in a black pot over the fire, and she smiled to recall one old man from the Kerry hills who would put his head in the door and shout, "Mary, have you any trough empty?"

All was changed now, however, with endless hot water on tap and French and German accents blending with the soft Kerry brogue.

Stepping into the warm oily bath was a soft poultice to the mind and body; the floating seaweed touched my skin like the caressing fingertips of a black lover. Suffused in the moist, steamy little world, I listened to the rain beat on the galvanised tin roof and to the sound of the waves as they crashed on to the beach outside. It was almost like a return to the womb. The cubicles on either side of me were unoccupied, so there was no sound but the rain and the sea, and I drifted off to sleep. I awoke to the noisy clatter of two Dublin women coming into the cubicles on either side of me. They were obviously good friends and carried on a conversation over my head as the dividers in the cubicles were not ceiling-high. Both husbands, who were out playing golf in the rain, were discussed in detail, so much so that before the bath water had cooled, I felt that I had got to know Tony and Aidan very well.

The conversation then turned to the musical society they belonged to, and almost as if an unseen choir master had raised his baton, they both burst into song and rendered the drinking song from *La Traviata* in high, clear voices. I wished that I had a glass of chilled white wine to drink a toast to these two flamboyant, light-hearted ladies, but instead I turned on the hot tap and leaned back to enjoy this unexpected concert. Their repertoire was entertaining and varied, but when they broke into "Goodbye" from *The White Horse Inn*, I took it as the finale and stepped out of the cooling seaweed bath.

After dinner that night, the rain having cleared, I set out to walk along the cliff-top to the Nine Daughters Hole and the Virgin Rock. High above the incoming tide was a seat, so I sat there to watch the sea. I have always had a love-hate relationship with the sea, feeling sometimes that it has hypnotic powers that could draw one down into it. Silently one of my teenage sons slipped on to the seat beside me. Unusually for him he sat wordlessly gazing out to sea. After a while he said quietly, "Nanna is slowing down, isn't she?"

Surprised, I looked into his young, troubled face and said lightly, "Do you think that she should be riding a bike around the strand?"

We both laughed and his face cleared. He was more sensitive to the shadows of old age than I had thought. We continued our walk, he threatening to throw me into the Nine Daughters Hole, which I ran past quickly as I heard the waves thundering in and out below.

Then we came to the little inlet known as the Nuns' Strand, its entrance guarded by the gigantic Virgin Rock. A convent perched on this cliff-top gave the sheltered beach its name. Here the nuns bathed in the days when they did not share our world, before Vatican II opened the door between us. The Virgin Rock guarded their beach and I wondered had its name anything to do with the proximity of the convent. We sat with our backs to the wall and watched the sea roll in to the beach below us. The Virgin Rock, shaped like the lower half of a human body, had its hips and vaginal regions washed by the swirling waves. As we watched, the light faded and the sea changed colours and then the Clare lighthouse flashed across the water through the gathering darkness. The first day of our holidays was drawing to a close, and I felt myself relaxing back into Ballybunion like a hand into a well-worn glove.

THE NUNS' STRAND

The smooth sea swirls silently,
Lapping with a deep, quiet calm
Against the dark-faced headland,
Which opens a deep mouth,
And the soft white waves
Roll with a soothing monotony
Along its sandy tongue
Over the giant jaw-bone,
Leaving traces of yellow spittle
Around its black grinders.

AUNTY MARY'S HANDBAG

S HE CONSTANTLY ASSURED me that my children were badly reared and my husband badly trained. Husbands, to Aunty Mary, were in the same league as colts and puppies: they needed to be broken in and house-trained. She considered herself to be an authority on husband management and child rearing, and because she had neither husband or children there was no way that I could prove to her that her theories did not work in practice. She tried to convince me that the only reason her ideas did not work for me was because I did not see them through with sufficient determination. She had never been made pliable by the moulding demands of husband and children and was free to devote her entire life to acting as a marriage advisory counsellor to the extended family. In every pool of relatives there is one who creates ripples, and Aunty Mary was the one who kept our pool alive.

She visited us regularly and told us everything we did not want to hear. To bring a visit to a grand finale, she often left in a storm of protest after a blazing row with Aunty Peg. These two sisters were both strong-minded women and sometimes when they came together "the fur flew", as Aunty Mary herself described it, but she was always the one to give the first tug. By nature controversial, she enjoyed swimming against the tide. She firmly believed that it was a woman's privilege to change her mind constantly, and as she practised what she preached, Aunty Mary's tide was for ever flowing in different directions.

In the early days of my marriage, when Aunty Peg considered me to be far short of perfect, Aunty Mary championed my cause and declared me to be a wonderful addition to the family circle. Over the years, however, as Aunty Peg and I became good friends, Aunty Mary changed her mind and decided that maybe I was after all a bit of a disaster. She was totally unpredictable and so one could never anticipate what stance she would take in any situation. But she had one great virtue in that she never nursed a grudge. It was not that she was all-forgiving but simply that she forgot. Once the storm was over she set her sails in another direction and was ready for the next challenge.

She was a wonderful cook, but as the temperature in the kitchen rose, so did Aunty Mary's temper. But because she was such a genius in the kitchen, she was in great demand by top-class hotels where she reigned supreme. She worked during the summer months only and rested for the winter, when she visited all the family and gave us the benefit of her advice. She seldom worked in the same hotel for two successive seasons, because she never finished a term without telling the manager or owner how they should be running the establishment. Even if asked to return, she seldom did so as she liked a change of scene.

At the beginning of every summer it was our job to drive her to the hotel of her choice for that season. Sometimes we were summoned to make a hasty return if there was an immediate clash of temperament with a manager who would not fall into line with Aunty Mary's way of thinking. She had a very low opinion of the male species, and when a bachelor brother, with whom she had lived, died and did not leave her his house, she felt that her opinion had been vindicated. It was not the loss of the house that upset her as much as the satisfaction she would have got from promising it to different members of the family and constantly changing her will. It would have provided an excellent source of entertainment in her old age.

As she grew older she became a dedicated hypochondriac, and her large black handbag grew into a mobile pharmacy. The bag was so big that in its earlier years it might have been an elegant overnight case, but those times were long gone, and in its later days it developed the contours of an overweight man trying to fit into boyhood clothes. It bulged and stretched to accommodate all Aunty Mary's medical needs, and when she had them packed in she snapped the two ancient brass bars together across the top and the two brass clasps locked into each other. It defied the laws of measured capacity in that it actually held all that was forced into it. It was packed with plastic phials and little glass bottles guaranteed to cure insomnia, headaches, indigestion, blood pressure and a multitude of complaints imaginary and otherwise. Some of the tablets were her own but many she had collected from friends and relatives over the years. She had a mania for collecting other people's left-over medicines and passed on her cures to anyone willing to receive them. From her many visits to various doctors, she considered herself to be a semi-professional and was anxious to practise her expertise on any guinea pig who came her way. If, on the other hand, a doctor or nurse happened to cross her path, they were a mine of untapped information that had to be quarried.

Once when she was on one of her visits to us, my friend Frances, a nurse, called to see her. To Aunty Mary it was a golden opportunity, so she took over the kitchen to conduct a medical conference and enter into a general analysis of her handbag. In the course of the consultation, she poured the entire contents of her mobile medical chest on to the large kitchen table. Out poured a colourful waterfall of little bottles and containers sparkling with bright red, yellow, green and white tablets. Frances surveyed this phenomenon with unbelieving horror etched into every line of her face. Aunty Mary demanded that she identify all the tablets and advise on the dosage to be taken. Frances was experiencing a situation which in the controlled world of hospital life would have been unthinkable. I walked away and left her to the mercy of Aunty Mary, who was like a cat with a fat mouse in her clutches.

Many hours later Frances came to me with a glazed look on her face. "I never saw the likes of it," she declared.

"Of what?" I asked innocently.

"That woman's handbag," she answered in a voice filled with horror.

"What's wrong with it?" I queried.

"There's enough tablets in there to kill half the parish," she announced. "They could blow the head off her."

"How?" I asked.

"She's taking too many tablets, and most of them are for complaints that she hasn't even got."

"But she's been doing that for years," I said.

"But she has even got morning sickness tablets in there!" my friend protested.

"I'm sure that they won't do much harm at this stage," I assured her.

"Well," Frances declared, "she must have the constitution of a horse, because what she is doing should be lethal."

Despite the pronouncement, Aunty Mary proceeded merrily on her way. During her visits she tried to introduce "law and order" into our house.

Because she was a dedicated cook, meals got priority consideration in her world, and she believed that when a meal was ready everybody in the house should drop whatever they were doing and all sit down together. With a shop attached to our house, that was impossible in our lives; we ate in relays and meals were movable feasts. This casual approach to eating annoyed her intensely and she assured me regularly that I ran a very *"trína chéile"** house. Never having been accustomed to having children around her, she could not understand the confusion of a home full of children, some of them noisy teenagers. She proclaimed them to be bad-mannered and badly behaved and told them and me that regularly.

For their part they took her in their stride, having been used to her coming and going all their lives. However, she stretched her luck and their patience to breaking point one year when, just as the All-Ireland Hurling Final was about to begin, she announced that lunch was ready and promptly turned off the television. They knew if they opposed her she would get the better of them by turning on her hearing aid, which could give out a piercing shrill whistle and drown the sound of the television. So they gulped down her beautifully prepared lunch with no sense or word of appreciation. We came home that night from Dublin to a state of cold war.

Her hearing aid was the bane of her life and a cause of constant frustration, which she often used

* *Mixed-up, confused*

to her advantage. If you were telling her something that she did not want to hear, she promptly turned it off and you finished up talking to yourself. Sometimes, thinking that she had it turned off, you might shout at her, only to be asked in annoyance, "Do you think that I'm deaf or something?"

She was for ever tampering with her hearing aid, which caused it to do things that no hearing aid should do. Sometimes, when it was supposed to be turned off, it sent out ear-piercing whistles which would put the hair standing on top of your head. When this happened in the middle of the night, somebody had to get out of bed and go to her room to "turn Aunty Mary off", while she slept peacefully through the whole racket. Despite all the trials and tribulations she inflicted upon us, one had to admire her because she had great spirit. When she arrived she took complete control of the kitchen and ran it like an army barracks. She laid down the law and we all fell into line.

She seldom stayed more than a week, because a week was as long as she could stand us. Then she donned her dark green velour hat and boarded the bus for home. However, as she grew older, her visits grew longer. Finally, when she became too old to be on her own, she came to stay permanently. We gave her a bedroom on the ground floor to spare her the effort of climbing the stairs. At first she came back and forth to the kitchen and lectured us when she felt we were getting out of hand, but gradually she became unable to do even that and stayed in bed completely.

In case we would not be able to hear her in the kitchen if she called, I gave her an old brass bell to summon help. I should have known better! Aunty Mary with a loud brass bell at arm's length was in her element. My God, but she used that bell! She was like the bells of Shandon, but instead of ringing on the half hour she rang almost non-stop. Even my neighbour from across the street wanted to know what the blazes was going on. Aunty Mary was delighted with her clanging bell and having given it to her there was no way I could take it off her.

She became obsessive about colds and draughts. Her room, which was quite small, was warmed by a large heater and she had an electric blanket and two hot water bottles. When you opened the door you were met by a wall of heat and sitting with her was like having a sauna. Changing her hot water bottles became the theme tune of her days. The bell rang constantly with requests to change them. Even when they were too hot to handle she wanted them changed. One of the children who became tired from journeying back and forth to the kitchen with the bottles devised a plan to limit the journeys. He would take them out into the corridor, where he would sit down quietly. Then, when he felt that a sufficient amount of time had elapsed, he would take them back in to her again. She never noticed the difference. The windows had to be kept firmly closed, and she complained of draughts coming from every direction, even out of the wardrobe. One evening after a long day of bell ringing, I stood in the kitchen grasping the two hot bottles and said to myself, "Alice, which will you do: laugh or scream?"

When I went back to her room with the two bottles I had to laugh because she pulled a bottle of whiskey out from under the bed saying: "Alice, will you take that bloody bottle of whiskey and make us two strong ones?"

"That's a great idea," I told her.

"There is only one way to handle this blasted old age," she declared, "and that's with a bottle of holy water in one hand and a bottle of whiskey in the other."

She had a restless spirit and had always been free to go when the spirit moved her, so now it was very constricting for her to be confined to one room. She vented her frustration on anyone unlucky enough to come at the wrong time. Visiting relatives could never be sure of their reception as it depended on the prevailing mood. One old cousin whom she did not like very much came to see her. She was asleep as I ushered him into the room, but she opened one eye as he sank heavily into a chair by her bed.

"Who's that?" she demanded, though I was convinced that she already knew because she had been prophesying his arrival.

"It's Mick," he announced.

"What brought you?" she demanded.

"I came to see you, Mary," he told her.

"You could have spared yourself the trouble then," she assured him.

"I heard you weren't well," he told her.

"You mean you heard that I was dying," she snapped at him.

"I did not," he assured her.

"You did so," she insisted, "because you would not be here otherwise. You were always a coffin chaser."

"Mary," he said, changing tactics, "there is nothing wrong with dying."

"No," she told him, "as long as it's not you that's doing it."

I decided to withdraw and let them at it, but I had hardly reached the kitchen door when Mick caught up with me and shot past me with a face like thunder, muttering about "that cantankerous old bitch". Aunty Mary was in great form for the rest of the day because she had won that battle. She never lost her fighting spirit.

When our local doctor told me that she could go very quickly, I really did not take him very seriously. But time proved him right. It was late one evening when a certain quietness came over her and the bell no longer rang. Frances, who years previously had been confounded by Aunty Mary's handbag, called in and we sat with her. Frances had always told me that she was only good at two things in life: making a good curry and comforting people in their last hours. Whatever about the curry, she there and then justified her second claim. She was a revelation to watch. She held Aunty Mary's hand and talked to her in a soft soothing voice. As she gently massaged the dying woman's face and eased her hair back from her forehead you could see the tension leave Aunty Mary and all the wrinkles of old age fade away. When she died peacefully a few hours later, her face had shed the ravages of time and she looked as she must have done as a young girl. She was tranquil and beautiful. It was one of the most extraordinary changes that I had ever seen. I knew that it would have given Aunty Mary immense satisfaction to carry off her final scene looking so well that even Mick would not have the satisfaction of saying otherwise.

After she had died I looked around the room and decided that the wall inside the bed could do with a lick of paint. I went out to the back porch for a tin of white paint and a brush. Balancing myself on the edge of the bed I leaned in over Aunty Mary and painted the wall above her. As I leaned across her, I could almost hear her say, "Alice, I always said that you had a *trína chéile* house!"

That night we had a surprise visit from a priest friend of ours who was home from Africa, and the following day he said Aunty Mary's funeral mass. Because he had not known her, he assumed that she had been a dear, gentle old lady who had accepted with resignation the frailties of old age. As he waxed eloquent about her many virtues I sensed that all around me her relatives, including Mick, were listening in amazement, wondering if they were at the wrong funeral. Even in death she could spring a surprise.

A Little Bit of Writing

"A LWAYS LIKED THE bit of writing," the old man told me. His eyes were so full of laughter that it overflowed and ran down his face, curling his mouth into a smile of mischievous innocence.

"Kept me out of harm's way," he continued, chuckling deep down in his angular frame. "Herself liked it, too," he added, and for a fleeting moment a shadow crossed his face. "She died at thirty-eight and there was only myself and the five little girls. Great little girls they were, all under nine years of age, but we managed together. Every night when we had the lessons done, we did the bit of writing and they enjoyed it. I worked on the road with the County Council and the girls were good at the schooling and got good jobs. Went to Dublin, the five of them, to the Civil Service and teaching. And do you know something: we often write to each other in verse because we all like the little bit of writing."

It was the opening night of Listowel Writers' Week and I was chatting to a craggy countryman in the ballroom of the Listowel Arms Hotel. This kindly-faced man from the Kerry hills stretched out his long legs and relaxed amidst the cheese and wine and pulsating music of the band that had couples young, middle-aged and ageless writhing to its rhythm.

Earlier that evening a friend and I had driven into the sun-soaked town, where a scattering of cars were parked in front of the hotel and a dog dozed outside the door. Yellow rambling roses draped around the windows gave the hotel the restful elegance of a country mansion. Our comfortable bedroom was on the first floor, looking out over the town square which was guarded by two steeples. My friend and companion for the week was a lady who believed in "bring it in case you'd want it", and by the time we had finally installed ourselves, we were in need of refreshments. We were joined in the bar by a Listowel man who was also attending Writers' Week, and he welcomed us to his town and wished us a pleasant stay.

Afterwards we walked up the town in search of a screw-in bulb for the light over one of the beds. It had blown just as I had pressed the switch, but rather than request a replacement at the now busy reception desk, we decided to use it as an excuse to take a walk around and get to know the town. Many of the shops were still open, and we spent a pleasant hour chatting to the friendly shop people. A screw-in bulb eluded us, however, but its importance diminished as the conversation developed.

Arriving back at the hotel, we made our way to the packed ballroom where Writers' Week was officially

opened. The attendance was assured that they could
be high brow, low brow, or no brow: Listowel catered
for them all. An elegantly attired ladies' choir took
us to musical heights, and Dan Keane, with his soft
Kerry brogue, chaired the occasion with droll wit. At
the door coming in we had been furnished with two
tickets, one for bread and one for wine, but there the
religious connotations severed as the crowd danced
happily into the small hours.

The following morning I made my way to the boys'
school which housed my choice of workshop. The
interchange of ideas between all the participants
made me realise that the workshop was a real mixed
bag of people. There were some Americans and
English, and the Irish people present were mainly
from the North of Ireland and Dublin. The Americans were exuberant and had no inhibitions about
reading their own works. The English spoke in BBC
accents, and I could see that they took this whole
workshop business very seriously. I was beginning to
think that maybe I had bitten off more than I could
digest when a light-hearted Dublin man read a very
funny short story he had written, and the whole
room rang with laughter.

Some people there had published work and were
anxious to polish their techniques, others were keen
to be published, others just enjoyed writing – if they
got published that was an extra bonus – and some
were there for the fun. A large man who sat beside
me scarcely opened his mouth for the first few days,

which made me extremely nervous; when I attempted-
ed conversation, he peered out over his rimless
spectacles at me as if I were talking nonsense – a possibility I did not entirely rule out. It had got to the
stage where I was afraid to open my mouth, because
when I am nervous I babble. One day, because he
had no choice, he read a short story he had written.
It was sad, sensitive and beautiful. When he had finished reading, some of the people in the workshop
had tears in their eyes. His story merited a round of
applause and he was dreadfully embarrassed. I was
amazed that such a grumpy, arrogant man, as I had
thought him to be, could have written such a story,
and I couldn't resist telling him so.

"But," he protested, "I'm not arrogant, just terrified. I was so nervous coming to this workshop that
I decided to keep a low profile."

"You certainly succeeded," I told him. "I was
scared stiff to open my mouth to you after my first
few attempts."

A big smile lit up his face and from then on we
enjoyed the workshop and each other's company.
As the workshop unfolded with the days, it became
apparent that it was sometimes the most retiring
in the group who were the talented ones. But the
variety of people present made me realise that the
urge to write spans all barriers, and as we relaxed
and came to know each other better, we got great
enjoyment out of our week together.

Apart from the workshops, the days in Listowel

offered a variety of readings, book launches, talks and drama. The happenings were spread all around the town, in the library, the hall, St John's church, the school and the pubs. In order to attend every function it would have been necessary to have winged feet. I was intrigued by one elderly nun who could have been clocking eighty and who was present at every event. We christened her the flying nun.

Our minds were stirred by a talk in the library on the poets of North Kerry, while in St John's church Sam McAughtry gave an unchurchlike and very amusing talk. He read from his works and opened our minds to the ordinary lives of the Protestant community in Northern Ireland and the humour that enables people to live together despite the continuing violence.

In the hotel ballroom Bob Kingdom took us on a mental journey to Wales and brought alive the beauty and cutting wit of Dylan Thomas. We were almost afraid to clear our throats lest we miss a gem-laden line. A mother with a gurgling baby in arms waving a plastic rattle had drifted in but felt compelled to bow out. Dylan Thomas shared centre stage with no one.

So packed was the schedule that there was hardly time to eat. People from the different workshops mixed and chatted in the hotel and in the pubs, where impromptu concerts and poetry readings developed. Mid-week a literary pub crawl led by a bodhrán player did the rounds, each pub staging a literary event, but towards the end of the night the literary vision of all concerned had become a little blurred. We did not see bed until the small hours of the morning, as people gathered in groups to discuss the different events and sometimes impromptu readings and long discussions followed. One American couple told me that they came to Listowel for Writers' Week every year. They did not join any workshop and they did not write; they just enjoyed being there for that week.

One night we were in a pub full of locals who had no interest in Writers' Week. One lad told me that he felt that it had no relevance to him, so a lively discussion on Irish attitudes evolved which the whole pub got stuck into. I asked him if he thought that he was "a hurler on the ditch"; to which he replied, "No, a footballer; you're in Kerry now, you know." He sat on his high stool and sang "The Old Bog Road" in a beautiful tenor voice and with such feeling that an old man beside me, who had come from England for Writers' Week, wiped a tear from his eye. When someone else sang a lively number, the same lad tapped out the rhythm on the counter with a long ice-tongs.

The pretty barmaid reached out, saying, "Give me that."

"That's a dangerous weapon," he cautioned, waving it over her head.

"It's not the only dangerous weapon you have," she told him sharply, gripping the tongs firmly and taking it off him. She was young, confident and pleasant, and served the entire pub with great assurance, deftly managing a bedraggled drunk whom she soothed with the right word whenever he was getting out of hand. At closing time the lad off the high stool collected the drunk and took him home.

It had been an enjoyable night during which poetry was read, songs sung, and debate, conversation and arguments ranged from writing and country lore to love making and the curse of emigration, from which many present had suffered.

A historic tour of North Kerry displayed many aspects of Kerry life, including its tolerance. Our bus driver parked in the middle of a crossroads and passing motorists – or, rather, motorists unable to pass – took it all in their stride with no sign of impatience. Not one blaring horn broke the silence of that beautiful countryside.

The highlight of the tour was the unveiling of a plaque on the home of Maurice Walsh, which was performed with dignity, eloquence and the colour of Kerry wit. The only hitch, ironically enough, was provided by a small, dark man with a greasy cap who took up his position beside the plaque, where he contrasted vividly with the whitewashed gable end of the cottage. He felt the need to give a running commentary on proceedings and, because of his somewhat unusual appearance and choice of words, was in danger of turning the whole proceedings into a one-man comic act. However, he proved no problem to his resourceful friends, because while Dan Keane engaged him in conversation, the powerful figure of Sean McCarthy stood in front of him and obliterated the little man from our view. There was no hassle; he was one of their own and belonged there, so they did nothing to upset him. A Kerry solution to a Kerry problem.

Over the door was a giant key depicting *The Key Above the Door*, a book which must have found its way into almost every home in Ireland. The key was crafted by local man Michael Barry who every Christmas helps to bring out the Ballydonoghue parish magazine. Writing flows through the veins of Kerry, and maybe Brendan Kennelly wrote the truth when he had Maloney say that it was in the Listowel water supply. From the area around Maurice Walsh's home came the ancestors of John B. Keane, Brendan Kennelly and Sean McCarthy. There must have been something special in that stretch of countryside.

There, in a little roadside thatched pub with an open turf fire and black crane, we had drinks and sandwiches. On a small, deep-set side window, a soundless television had its American soap opera obliterated when set dancers took to the floor and live music filled the pub. One woman who had previously played the bodhrán with gusto now hopped off the floor, the rhythm of the music controlling every movement of her body. When asked if it was a hard floor to dance on, she answered with flushed face and sparkling eyes, "It fights against you, but that's good, and the music intoxicates me."

Sean McCarthy shook the rafters with his rendering of "Rattle up the pots and the old tin cans" and his hilarious stories filled the day with laughter. Dan Keane traced the genealogy of every family home along the route back almost to Adam. That man had such a capacity for tracing family trees that Americans looking for their roots should run bus tours to him.

The literary giants of Listowel knit Writers' Week together and a small and dedicated team do trojan work. Gabriel Fitzmaurice, Chairman of Writers' Week, seemed to be everywhere; with bundles of papers hanging out of his pockets, he laced all the events together. Then late one night he gave a poetry reading upstairs in a back room of the Listowel Arms. His rich voice took us on a journey to many places, but we wound up looking into dark brown bog-holes and exploring the beauty of a child's mind. He spends his days with children and the child in him has never died.

The genial Bryan MacMahon walked the streets of Listowel during Writers' Week like a host at a large party. He welcomed newcomers and introduced them to locals, and while it was understandable that he knew everybody in Listowel he also seemed to know everybody who had come there for the week as well. The Writers' Week was his brainchild and now that his child had become a mature adult he was enjoying the fruits of his labours. He then told me about the night he had come home from Dublin when Listowel had won the All-Ireland Drama competition. He had danced in delight around his mother's kitchen and she had advised, "Bryan, walk easy when your jug is full." He laughed now as he recalled her advice and then he took us into a little tea-room where we had tea and buns.

Who but John B. would silence the crowd and sing "The Banks of My Own Lovely Lee" to welcome us to his pub? He sat on a high stool outside the counter and regulated a continual concert, insisting that each artist was awarded respectful silence. If his requests did not penetrate to those minds intent on other business, his sons imparted his instructions to them and his charming wife Mary supervised behind the counter. Like a king on a throne, John B. was monarch of all he surveyed. On a stool beside him sat a small brown man like a wren on top of a holly bush. From his elevated position we were at eye level.

"Have you a chirp in you?" he demanded.

It took me a few seconds to interpret his enquiry as to my singing ability, which for the sake of the common good has to be confined to the privacy of home. Soon a girl with a beautiful, clear lilt brought absolute silence. The following morning at mass the same voice filled the church with its beauty. She definitely had more than "a chirp" in her. She was the dawn chorus.

At breakfast that morning we were joined by two native Irish speakers from Dingle, one of whom I had met previously. As my Irish was not too fluent they were forced into English, which did not come easy to one of them. His friend remarked jokingly, "This fellow is half illiterate: he has only one language."

To which the other man declared, "At least I'm only illiterate in one language. You're illiterate in two."

He went on to tell me about an old parish priest who had been in Dingle when he was young.

"He would always doze off in the confession box, but if you mentioned girls or sins of the flesh, he would straighten up and cock his ear and ask for every detail. The only sexual experience that man ever had was in through his ear."

He continued earnestly, "Priests should get married, I think. Do you know something: it is my belief that God did not give us any spare parts."

It was a most entertaining breakfast, laced as it was with Dingle theology.

As we left the hotel we met Eamon Keane. Having listened to his wonderful voice on radio over the years, he was somebody for whom I had the greatest admiration. His dark brooding eyes in his thin ascetic face gave him the appearance of a medieval monk. He told me that he was meeting an old friend for lunch; they had gone to school together and been childhood sweethearts but had not met for over thirty years.

"What will she think of me now?" he mused gently.

"I think that she will fall in love with you all over again," I told him, and looking at his dark, handsome, sensitive face, I felt that it would not be too difficult for any woman.

As we left Listowel I remembered the advice his mother had given to Bryan MacMahon and felt that after our week there all our jugs were a little fuller.

HIDDEN POET

You live behind
The mirror of a
Carefree, laughing boy.
But you are an
Old old woman
Whose sensitive eyes
Have seen too much,
Whose vulnerable heart
Has bled too much.
You hide it
Behind your mirror,
Which once cracked,
Revealing for a moment,
The sad soul of
A poet.

GENTLE JESUS

THEY DECIDED ON impulse to come to our village. One day as David had driven through it, he had thought that it would be a nice place to live. His job did not tie them to any particular location, and within a week they had moved into a little house up the street from my own. David was a good-looking, easy-going Kerryman, with a quicksilver mind, who enjoyed fishing and reading, but Rachel was the one who drew all eyes in her direction. Her father was from the west of Ireland, her mother from France, and she was beautiful. David called her his Botticelli woman; she was voluptuous and well endowed, and folds of brown curling hair cascaded down around her shoulders. But it was her face that really held your attention; it was oval shaped with dark brown eyes and her skin was tawny with golden freckles. She was the most relaxed easy-going person I ever met and her rich, husky voice flowed over you like soothing cream. I always felt on meeting her that she had time for everything and that she never bothered with the word hurry – it was not in her vocabulary. They were a wonderful couple and it was obvious that they were at peace with each other and with the world.

They had three young, dark-eyed children – a boy and two girls – and the boy became the bosom pal of one of our children. He often stayed with them at night and absolutely adored Rachel; when he came home to tell me on one occasion that he wished she was his mother, I had to agree that he showed great wisdom in his choice. I was told that if the children wanted pancakes after going to bed, then Rachel made pancakes and joined them in bed to eat them. Part of David's job involved long hours on night duty and Rachel was happy to spend all her time with the children. Their garden ran down to the banks of the river. Rachel and the children spent hours swimming there and she taught the village children to swim. After a few months in their house up the street, a farmhouse became available outside the village and they moved into it. They were delighted with the freedom of the fields and the children grew browner. When Rachel became pregnant again, she wore her pregnancy with a regal cloak and glowed with good health.

The night the baby was born, David called to tell us that he had Down's syndrome. In the weeks that followed, you could see that they were bowed but not broken. They called the little lad Johnny. A month later David inherited a farm from an uncle in a very remote part of Kerry and they moved from Innishannon.

Ten years later I was sitting in a restaurant in Listowel during Writers' Week. At a table across from me with his back to me sat a man whom I thought was vaguely familiar. During the meal I glanced occasionally in his direction, trying to place him in my memory, but as I could not see his face it proved impossible. But when he stood up to leave there was no mistaking the dark hair and the laughing eyes: it was David. We were thrilled to see each other again after so many years and we spent all our free time for the rest of the week catching up with each other's news. I promised that when we would be in Ballybunion later that summer we would drive out to see them.

The sun was blazing down behind the Virgin Rock as we left Ballybunion with our eight-year-old daughter Lena in the back seat and we set out for their house. Lena had never met a Down's syndrome child, and I wondered if I should prepare her with an explanation. I did not want her to do or say anything that would upset David and Rachel. However, I could not find the right words, so I kept my mouth shut.

When David had said that their house was "a bit out of the way", he had not been exaggerating. After leaving behind a small town, we passed occasional houses for a while, but then for a long time there were only hills and sea; the road turned into a track and I was beginning to think that we were on the road to nowhere when suddenly we saw it in the distance. A house clung to the sea front, and in fields around it sheep and horses grazed, looking at us as in disdain when we approached and disturbed the silence. One pony in particular stood out, with his long flowing mane and rich colouring. Dogs bounced out to greet us, but we could not find the front door as the house seemed to face in all directions, and then David came from another direction and ushered us in.

Inside Rachel sat in a huge old armchair, slightly more ample and with a few grey hairs, but as beautiful as ever, and her gorgeous husky voice was like warm honey. The room was full of books and comfortable disorder, and a fire glowed in an amazing stone fireplace. Rachel had collected the stones on the beach, especially after winter storms which had blown up new varieties, and had built it herself. It was obvious that she loved living by the sea, and David told us that Johnny had been reared with the same feeling and was an expert swimmer. They talked of their horses as part of the extended family and of one pony in particular who had a long flowing mane and had been christened by the children "Gentle Jesus". Remembering the beautiful pony outside, I thought that he was aptly named, because there was something almost angelic about him. His temperament, however, they told us, did not exactly match his appearance, so there was a touch of irony about his name.

Quietly the door opened and Johnny stood there. He sized us all up with a happy smile on his face and then walked straight over to me and climbed on my lap. He put his arms around my neck, looked straight into my eyes and then said in a breathless voice, "Aren't you beautiful?"

Needless to mention, he had me in the palm of his hand after that. He was the most lovable child and wanted you to know that you were welcome in his house. He took Lena by the hand and they went out happily to play in the sand.

As we talked it was easy to see that even though Johnny had brought certain problems he had also brought immense joy to the family. They had surrounded him with great love and assurance of his importance, and Rachel was now teaching in the special school that he attended. The rest of the children were grown up and working away from home. But Johnny went to them on holidays, even flying out on his own to be met by them at airports.

It was the early hours of the morning as we drove down the bumpy path from their house. Lena in the back seat was silent for a little while and then she leaned over the back of my seat and said, "Wasn't that house full of love and wasn't he a very special little boy?"

Silently I thanked God that I had kept my mouth shut earlier on and not coloured with my adult inhibitions what she with her child's vision had so aptly described. As we left their farm behind, I looked back and Gentle Jesus was grazing peacefully with the sheep.

SPECIAL CHILD

With soft hands you caressed my hair
And touched my face with child kisses;
Looking into your eyes of love
I saw inside
The tabernacle of the Lord.
Special child, you are so loved
That no earthly doubts
Have touched your saintly essence,
Leaving heaven's gate ajar
You live within a beam
Untouched by man.
May the world move gently with you
As you walk above its roughness.

TEA AND TOAST

THE NEED AROSE in me before going to Lough Derg or into the labour ward to paint my toenails a bright, dazzling scarlet. On one occasion it was to look up at them and on the other to look down. These were the two occasions in life which I really felt tested my endurance. However, on the night before my last visit to Lough Derg, I decided that maybe I could manage without my ten red flags, so I cast aside my bottle of nail varnish. In a moment of false courage a few months previously, when the CIÉ circular had come by post, I had lifted the phone and booked a ticket. Viewed from the long time distance of two months, Lough Derg did not look so threatening, and once booked I put it out of my mind. Ostrich-like I buried my head in the sand.

Many years previously I had come across Lough Derg when, as innocent teenagers, a friend and I set out to spend a weekend on an island. We scarcely knew its name, but we had a vague idea that the food might not be so good. Dressed in cotton dresses, we travelled up by bus in glorious sunshine with not a warm garment between us. To say that we got a shock would be an understatement. Paralysed with cold, starved with hunger and blinded from lack of sleep, we lurched around the island like two drunks. We were stunned by the unquestioning stupidity that had led us into this corner of crucifixion. The only distraction from misery was provided by two young men who, like ourselves, had found that things were not quite up to their expectations; we met them regularly to smoke cigarettes and swap funny stories. As I watched the other barefooted pilgrims praying, I thought that they should all be locked up. After that visit I never again wanted to see a cigarette and vowed that wild horses would not drag me back to that miserable place.

Over the years Lough Derg had hidden like a grey ghost in my subconscious. Later I began to wonder what it was really like. Buried as I had been in my own misery, I had not really sized it up or taken on its challenge. It had beaten me and I needed now to know why that had happened. So I went back, better prepared, and on my second visit it had shaken me but had not flattened me. And occasionally I returned again to that sombre little island, as unyielding as steel, which stretches you to the limit of your endurance.

This year as I packed my Lough Derg bag in the middle of a burning heatwave, I wondered if my usual island ensemble would be necessary. But a little wise remembrance from within cautioned that when God made Lough Derg he gave it a special weather zone. So in went a long-sleeved thermal vest and matching knickers. Brief panties have no role on the Lough Derg fashion ramp. Next I included a warm blouse, a pure wool polo-neck sweater and an extra heavy wool woven jumper, knowing that Lough Derg is the place to prove the difference between pure wool and synthetics. Then in went a warm track suit, army pants belonging to a teenage son that in ordinary circumstances I would not be seen dead in, and a pair of knitted tights with the soles cut off; after that a heavy duffel coat and a set of oils.

Some marketing people have based their sales technique on claims that their products have kept climbers warm on Everest, while hand-cream has been marketed with claims that it has been used to good effect by Nordic fishermen. I am waiting for the day that some wise Irish company will brand their goods "tested and proved on Lough Derg". Sun-tan oil, insect repellent and knitted gloves could all be necessary on one visit to that island, where the temperature can range from tropical to below zero within twenty-four hours.

That holy island is full of surprises, and sometimes they sneak up and trip you when you think that you have everything under control. One year Lough Derg might lull you into a false sense of security by being almost bearable. Then on the next unsuspecting visit, it might nearly murder you.

As I waited for the bus on that lovely warm

summer's day, a friend came along.

"Are you off for the day? You have a great life!" Little did she know.

The bus was full of women, which confirmed my opinion that we females are made of sterner stuff than the male. On the journey up we said some prayers that were slotted in between songs from the singers on the bus. It always surprises me that the people who do Lough Derg are generally light-hearted and happy.

That night we stayed in Bundoran and at my dinner table was a pretty, trendy teenager full of pep and sparkle.

"Have you been to Lough Derg before?" I asked.

"No," she answered brightly; "my mother was going but something turned up at the last minute and she couldn't go, so I'm coming instead."

"You'll be fine," I said encouragingly.

"Of course I will," she said in surprise, and I remembered my first visit and hoped that she would fare better than I had.

Later that night we had tea and biscuits before midnight, the last normal food for the next three days. It was unusual for me to have a large double bed to myself. As I lay there in solitary state, I felt like Queen Victoria. Bedroom television is not a home luxury, so I turned it on in anticipation, but the sexual activity in the late night movie was so intense that I got exhausted just watching. To preserve my energy for the days ahead, I switched it off and decided to go to sleep. The couple in the badly sound-proofed bedroom above did not, however, have sleep on their minds, and moans of pleasure rolled across my ceiling. Finally the sea of passion ebbed and we all got to sleep.

The following morning I decided to test the climatic conditions before dressing. I put my head out the bedroom window and had it nearly whipped off by a gale force wind. Lough Derg's icy fingers were reaching out for me. Breakfast was a glass of warm water. I watched other guests file in for breakfast, and as the smell of toast and bacon and egg wafted out of the dining-room, I swore that I would never again take such comforts for granted. The thought of a sizzling sausage made my teeth water, and my stomach groaned in sympathy. How could I be so crazy, I asked myself, to be subjecting myself to this madness? And this was only the beginning! I looked at the normal people and wondered where had I gone wrong. A vastly overweight man headed for the dining-room and I felt like grabbing him by the arm and inviting him to

Go mad along with me;
The worst is yet to be.

When we left the bus on the shore of Lough Derg, the temperature took a sudden dip. I made my way to one of the lakeside toilets and dug out extra clothes. Trying to undress in a toilet which was only meant to accommodate certain limited movements required the flexibility of a ballet dancer, but eventually I emerged, having inserted an extra layer of clothes beneath the top layer. I suspected that over the following days I would gradually pad outwards until my final outline would resemble a sumo wrestler.

Stepping into the wobbling boat, I regretted my armchair decision to leave the world for two days. The lake was dishwater grey; the boat was blue-grey; the island in the distance was white-grey and my mind was a dull grey. In contrast to the bleak surroundings, the people in the boat were laughing and good-humoured. But one woman with a coat draped around her shoulders sat gazing into space. Talking to herself, and maybe addressing the man in question, she asked sadly, "Jesus, what brought me here?"

But it was too late for such questions, so she smiled with resignation and determination. Lough Derg is not the place to approach with a negative frame of mind. We braced ourselves for the days ahead. As the boat chugged across the lake, the barren contours of the island rose up to meet us and its impressive grey stone buildings blended with water and sky. It was my first sight of the new hostel for women, which merged with the old buildings as if it had been there for hundreds of years. No plastic, chrome or glass building blights the landscape of Lough Derg. It is clothed in the austerity of medieval times. As I watched the island approach, my heart sank like a stone in a bucket of water and the thought of swimming for the mainland crossed my mind, but the dark grey water frowned back at me. There was no way out now.

Straight across from the landing bay is the large dome-shaped basilica and stretching out from it on either side are other grey buildings, which extend all around the edges of this small, barren island. They are like an encircling army and their centrepiece is a sloping mound in the middle of the island; here are the famous Lough Derg "beds", around which this island revolves. Bed in this case is a very misleading term, certainly not apt for the six stony circles of hardship riding on the back of that little hill in the centre of the island. Each bed has at its centre an iron cross embedded in rock with a stone path around it. Enclosing the cross and circular path is a stone wall and outside around that is another circular stone path. The six beds, each named after an Irish saint, lie like a drab patchwork quilt on the side of that hungry little hill which has its back to the lake and its face to the basilica.

Women's liberation came to Lough Derg before it hit the mainland, because St Brigid is at the top here. You start with her and you must watch your step as she is extremely steep and you could break your neck if you decided to rush her. Next comes St Brendan, who is to her right and slightly lower down where she can keep an eye on him. He is rough and edgy with treacherous spiked stones that could penetrate a hastily positioned toe; the secret here is careful, premeditated movement. Then comes St Catherine, who has a pathway of small, sharp, cruel stones, and then Columba who is easier. Next is St Patrick and finally the double bed of Davog and Molaise who, maybe because double beds are conducive to relaxation, lie in flat comfort under an overhanging tree on the water's edge. These little beds have lain here for centuries and thousands of barefoot pilgrims have walked and prayed over them. Sometimes the prayers are peppered with unpremeditated swearing as the bitter little stones extract their last drop of penitential hardship.

When we arrived at the hostel, we climbed up and up the stone stairway to the top floor which was divided into tiny cubicles, each holding bunk beds and a sink with a single cold water tap. We decided then on the amount of clothes necessary for the day, which was bitterly cold, so another layer went on and we took off our shoes. Bare feet are the common denominator of Lough Derg. On the first day the prescribed medicine is three beds. Now, "doing a bed" consists of the following routine: a visit to the basilica and then to St Patrick's iron cross, outside which you say one Our Father, Hail Mary, and Creed. Then to St Brigid's cross on the outside wall of the basilica, where you say three Our Fathers, three Hail Marys and one Creed, and then with your back to the wall of the basilica you stretch out your arms and publicly renounce the devil. The poor old devil gets a rough ride on Lough Derg! Everybody is trying to put the run on him. The first time you do this you feel a bit dramatic, and some people do it with an amused grin on their faces. It doesn't knock a shake out of the hardy annuals. Then you walk four times around the basilica and say seven decades of the rosary. After that it's on to the beds, starting at the top with St Brigid and the formula is the same for each bed. You walk around outside the low stone wall, kneel at the entrance, walk around inside, kneel at the cross at the centre and repeat the prayers that you said at St Brigid's cross. Preservation of your kneecaps and maintenance of balance is the aim of the game on those slippery, spiky slopes. Each pilgrim becomes an expert at balancing on one leg like a singing hen until a vacant space becomes available for the second foot. On some occasions one can find oneself reduced to going on all fours to get around a tight corner.

The next destination is the water's edge, where you increase the prayers from three to five and say them standing and kneeling. After that, it is back to the iron cross and you finish, as you began, in the basilica. It takes about an hour to do a bed, depending on your average speed. Some people plod around like contented cows in a world of their own. Others clock up prayers like a bandit making notches on his gun. As we had come early to the island, we had plenty of time to do our beds. When I had finished mine, I felt drained with exhaustion and hunger and thought longingly of home, where they would all be tucking into their tea. They were probably wondering how their crazy mother was surviving, and if they could have seen me they would have had a good laugh. The reason for doing Lough Derg was beyond their understanding and, at that stage, was beyond mine as well.

In the mid-afternoon the rain started to come down. Many of the teenagers were in jeans and sweaters and looked up reproachfully at the sky as if asking God what did he think he was doing. But at least their feet were free to enjoy the rain.

The variety of feet on Lough Derg tell an interesting story. The soft, perfectly formed feet of the very young flit over the stones like nimble hooves of mountain goats. Slightly older feet are still almost in their original condition, but are not quite as flexible on the rocks. Then come the older ones, branching out like gnarled trees into mature humps and bumps. But very old feet, like very old faces, are the most fascinating of all. They are like craggy rocks, some distorted into unusual shapes with varied toe formations and discoloured toenails. All these feet move over the beds, clambering, slipping, climbing and seeking level footholds. Some toes are bandaged, and the most touching sight of all are the feet of the women, no longer young, wearing elastic stockings which are covered at the heel with wet mud. The feet of Lough Derg are a touching, impressive sight. Sometimes, when the strong, bony toe of a mountainy man cracks against a spiked rock, a few extra prayers are said that were never heard in church.

Here in Lough Derg is a hidden core of our life that is difficult to analyse. It is as Irish as the brown bogs and grey mountains and is a living, breathing essence that still runs through our veins.

When we had our three beds done, we went for our meal. One is permitted daily, but meal, like bed, is a misleading term in this context. You are not confused by choice: black tea or coffee, dry toast and plates of Lough Derg biscuits, which are not eaten but gnawed. If you decided to take a bite, you could cause endless dental damage. I like a lot of milk in my tea and at the sight of the black tea my eyes sent a coded message to my queasy stomach to prepare for an unwelcome intrusion. The trick is to drink and not to think and to chew through as much dry toast as possible for future sustenance.

After tea there was mass at 6 o'clock, and here you became aware of strange sleeping companions. All during mass, heads dropped forward, overcome by sleep, and the sleepers were not very fussy about what shoulder they slept on. These were the unfortunates who had not been to bed at all the night before and were now exhausted from hunger and lack of sleep. After that mass we had a short rest; we donned another layer of clothes for the night and returned to the basilica looking like walking pillows. At 9.30 we had night prayers, after which the crowd dwindled to half as the people who had difficulty in staying awake went smilingly to bed.

It was then that our vigil began, and that's the

boy that tests your grit. During that long night we made four beds, but instead of outside, it was inside around the basilica, which was far more monotonous. The beginning of the night was not too bad, but as it got older so did we. It was a long, bitterly cold night, and as it wore on the hunger weakened us, the lack of sleep blinded us, the damp, freezing air penetrated our layers of clothes and my ankle and knee joints felt wooden. But I was not alone in my misery. As the night dragged on, surrounding faces paled and footsteps dragged. I had never realised that you could walk around sound asleep until I went to Lough Derg. Before that I had thought that only horses slept standing up. Between each bed we came outside for fresh air to wake us up and some brave souls washed their faces in cold water. If Lough Derg had not been an island, wandering souls would have been found making their ways homewards, but there was no escape. The cold black water lapped ominously against the shore and the mainland was a long way away.

I was gradually curling up into a hard knot of cold misery. At 4 a.m. I hit rock bottom and thought of a friend who had said, "Only the mentally ill go to Lough Derg."

At that point I agreed completely with him. Oh God, I thought; what brought me to this grey forsaken hole? But then the dawn broke, and as the grey light crept across the silent waters, I knew that the crisis point had passed.

For 6 a.m. mass the pilgrims after their night's sleep poured into the basilica and we who had been up all night mingled with them and tried to keep our eyes open. It was easy to tell us apart, for they were fresh-faced and smiling while we were grey-faced and bleary-eyed. During mass I hovered on the brink of unconsciousness and at one point thought that the priest was dancing along the altar rails. But instead of doing a slow-moving dance of the seven veils, he was jumping high off the rails in some high-flying jig and every time my dimmed vision connected with him he had gone higher, until in the end I thought that he was hanging off the ceiling. The man sitting next to me gave me a gentle nudge, which brought the high-stepping priest back down to earth. Sleep was the common enemy and people helped each other to stay awake. Finally the mass ended and we came out into the cold grey morning. Then we had two choices: to sit outside and freeze or sit inside and try to keep awake. We compromised by doing both at regular intervals. A long, long day stretched ahead. Oh, for breakfast in bed and a warm bath!

Confessions were next on the agenda and at least they broke the monotony. It was open-plan confession. Well distanced from each other inside the rails, a row of priests sat on chairs. We had a choice of a dozen priests, and I chose the one who had given the holy hour the night before because I liked his style. Some of the priests were young and good looking and they had a continuous stream of teenagers because they, too, shared the same wavelength. The pace was very leisurely. A restless lady next to me complained, "Some people are so slow, we'll be here all day."

I was tempted to ask her where was she planning to go. Instead I whispered back that maybe what people wanted as part of their pilgrimage here was to chat to one of the priests. She sniffed in annoyance and that conversation ground to a halt. When my turn came I had not intended to delay very long. But the priest was interesting and we got to talking about different things and time did not seem to matter. After me came the woman in a hurry and I hoped that the sunny-faced priest could slow her down. There was, after all, no point in rushing, for there was nowhere to go.

Just one bed had to be done that morning, and the aim for the rest of the day was simply to keep awake. We were lucky that the day had become warmer and we were able to sit outside where it was easier to keep awake. The obsession with personal misery was broken by the Stations of the Cross at 3 p.m.; it can only be on Lough Derg that one would look forward to the Stations of the Cross. As the sun rose higher in the sky and bore down on the exposed little island, the sun-tan lotion came into action; in the late evening the midges came out to play and had to be suitably repulsed. The midges on the island were a giant, blood-thirsty breed and, like the Mounties, they always got their man.

Lough Derg possesses a deep quietness. The only sounds to be heard are the lapping of lake water against rocks, the murmur of voices and occasional birdsong. No footsteps disturb the stillness. Transistors, televisions, phones and cameras are not allowed to intrude here. You are without shoes, without food, without sleep, and in the monotonous repetition of prayers, your mind is cleansed of all thoughts. Here your outer layers are stripped off. Your mind is cleared of clutter and you set aside all the things that were so important on the mainland. You have stepped off the world for two days and Lough Derg removes the dead layers of mental debris. It happens almost without your awareness, and as the second day draws to a close, you find an inner peace seeping into your being. If you so desire, you can chat to different people. Many come back again and again, finding here something that defies analysis. Maybe it is time out of life.

On the island that day there were over a thousand people. The accents of every county in Ireland mingled together and indeed some not Irish. In the basilica on that last night, I looked at all the different faces and wondered what kind of person came here, but there was no answer. The very old stun you with their tenacity; men and women with faces like hewn rocks; country people who have worked hard and prayed well all their lives. Others with golden, even tans acquired in warmer climates grip the rocks with well-manicured, multi-ringed fingers. Students imploring God for merciful examiners struggle with their first experience of exposure to cold and hunger. The young, the old, the middle-aged, from all walks of life, come to Lough Derg.

Going to bed that night was like going to heaven. Cold, sleepy and absolutely drained of stamina, we stretched out under the warm blankets. It was sheer, blissful ecstasy, and when the bell rang the following morning, I thought that I had only been in bed for a few minutes. After mass we made the final bed, but I had wings on my feet. As I stood at the water's edge on that sunny, sparkling morning saying the last prayers, a bird sang on a branch above me and it was as if my heart was singing with him.

Then we made our real beds in preparation for the people arriving on that day. We washed our feet, put on our shoes and normal clothes and went down to the pier to catch the boat to the mainland. Nothing was to be eaten that day except water biscuits and minerals. But we did not mind because it was all over and we were going home with quiet pools of peace in our hearts, a peace formed in the long hours away from the normal world.

NEEDS

Give me space
To roll out my mind,
So that I can open
The locked corners
Where lost thoughts
Are hidden.
I need time
In a quiet place
To walk around
The outer edges
Of my being,
To pick up,
Fragmented pieces,
To put myself
Back together again.

BIDDY'S BRIEF

TWO WOMEN STANDING outside my window were giving it their full attention. One, large and buxom with a headscarf knotted tightly under a row of double chins, stood with her arms resting on her hips, where they had ample accommodation.

"Would you take one look at that window," she demanded of her companion. "Isn't it a pure disgrace?"

"It is indeed, Biddy," her friend agreed. The companion was a direct contrast to Biddy. She was small, pale and wispy, with a look of perpetual agreement on her face.

"Wouldn't you think now that they would do something about it and they living on the side of the street where everyone can see them and all?" Biddy declared. "That house is a disgrace to the village and it right on the corner in the centre of everything. She can't be much of a housekeeper to have a window like that," she concluded.

They say that eavesdroppers never hear well of themselves, and Biddy had just proved the truth of that maxim, giving me an earful of something that

I did not want to hear. The fact that she was right made it all the more indigestible. The window in question, as well as the others along the front of our house, was in a sad condition. They had been installed at a time when architects had been going through a period of all window and no wall. The fact that Irish weather conditions were not exactly favourable to such wide-open thinking had not daunted their quest for glass menageries. Gradually the years had battered the window frames and loosened the louvres, and even though Biddy was no town planner, she had hit the nail on the head. We had been talking about doing something about those two front rooms for years, but the thought of turning the whole house upside-down made us put it off and off. It was not the windows alone that were the problem. We had badly fitting doors and rising damp, and to spend a night in our front rooms you needed leg warmers and thermal underwear. One of my sisters refused to come and stay after November 1 for fear that she might be frozen to death. She told me that our house was a health hazard and she was not referring to our lack of hygiene.

Now that Biddy had put her finger on the start button, we knew we had to make a move. The first step was to get the Protim man, who proved to be smart, efficient and to the point.

"These two rooms and the hallway will have to be stripped down to the stone. Then send for us and we will come and inject it. That will cure your rising damp," he said matter-of-factly, waving his hand in all directions. By the time all that would be done, I thought, I would be in need of an injection myself.

I mentioned my proposed renovations to the members of the family who were still in the nest and met with a mixed response.

"What's wrong with it the way it is?" remarked one unenthusiastic, unobservant student son.

Another smiled with delight. "Thank God," he said; "this place is like Siberia."

A third son pleaded, "Don't make it posh. I don't like posh houses that look as if nobody lives in them."

And my husband asked plaintively, "Do we have to turn the whole house upside-down again?"

This he said despite the fact that we had actually done nothing to it for the past twenty years.

Biddy had placed the bit between my teeth and now there was no holding me. First to be tackled was the furniture, which we had accumulated over the years when old relatives had died; it was battered and damaged and some of it had long been the home of geriatric woodworms. Storing it was going to be a problem. But over the years I had had several dilapidated chairs upholstered by Deaf Enterprises and they had given an excellent service, so in the morning I rang them and they said that they would come to collect. But first I had to empty the collection of years out of drawers and presses. The next week was spent on my hands and knees, surrounded by little boxes into which I sorted the kind of collection of useless debris that can only be accumulated in a family home occupied by a hoarding husband and a collection of like-minded children. If I threw anything away, it was bound to be needed the following day and to be of irreplaceable value.

By the time this job was done, I had developed a hump that almost brought my head parallel to my kneecaps. But it had an amusing side as well. I had unearthed dog-eared, blotched photographs of grinning toothless babies, which I waved under the noses of arrogant teenagers who thought that they had always been towering pillars of knowledge. Old newspaper cuttings of the local team were discovered and had to be brought to the kitchen table where the various players were identified. We were all surprised at how boyish the players looked in the old photographs and how they had changed. We almost expected to have fifteen Dorian Greys. The sorting out took longer than anticipated due to all the long-lost treasures I unearthed. Old newspapers that had lined the bottoms of drawers and lain there undisturbed for years could, I discovered, be very interesting.

Finally the last box was full and labelled. I had firmly donned my efficiency hat. My only hope of seeing this whole thing through was to hold on to it despite whatever gale-force wind of familial controversy might hit me over the following weeks.

The van arrived and the move started. First out was a bureau which had not functioned properly for years, its missing parts having spent a term buried under the stairs. It deserved the respect due to survival if nothing else. We had bought it on the way home from our honeymoon and I felt protective towards it because one of my sisters, on first sighting, had criticised its shape. She had christened it Bill Brennan, after an overweight friend of ours who had enormous lower regions and a narrow head and shoulders. Both our bureau and Bill Brennan, she had declared, were prime examples of bad design. Now we laid poor old Bill on the flat of his back in the van with his defunct parts across his front.

Next in was an old oak sideboard that Aunty Peg had bought when nobody was giving such things house room because the country was deep in the throes of bungalow bliss. Aunty Peg had no time for "new falderals", as she called them, and everything that she had was old. Over the years our children had spilled lemonade on top of it and the hinges had fallen off the doors; it was a picture of decayed elegance and an example of how children should not be reared. I entered the van with it to make sure that it was well placed and comfortable, so that its old joints would not be rattled.

Last in was an old couch that had suffered greatly beneath horse-playing teenagers. It had also been the temporary day-time bed for babies whom their optimistic mother had believed no longer needed nappies. Over the years my aching back had discovered its most comfortable sags and it had eased itself lovingly around tired muscles; sitting on it at the end of a long day had been like a reunion with an old friend. But now its bone structure was beginning to emerge and it was in need of internal uplift and some facial surgery.

Finally the van moved away and I stood and watched it out of sight. The contents of that van had shared my life, and I was flooded with guilt to be parting with them, even if it was for their own good. I felt almost as if I were sending my grandmother to the canning factory, and my mood was not improved when a neighbour called across to enquire, "Are you going into voluntary liquidation?"

Soon the sound of a sledge and kango hammer filled the house; grey dust rose like a fog and sneaked its way over everything, even into the cups in the kitchen. Eventually our old walls were bared to the stone and the Protim man returned to bore holes along the base and pump in green gunge. I pitied the mice and spiders who for years had roamed free between these stones.

We were filling in spaces around the windows and doors. Concrete blocks and sand and water moved in around us and large window spaces became normal window spaces. The usual wrangling with builders' suppliers took place and doors that were meant to have four panels arrived with six, but at this stage in my renovating career, I took details like that as part of the normal procedure.

While the building was going on, I was busy

working on colour combinations and driving the rest of the family crazy. My one-track mind was obsessively intent on restoring one small room into a tranquil corner free from television, radio or background music; a quiet room for sitting by the fire, reading and talking. I wanted to christen it the parlour, but was shot down by a smart son who told me that in today's world there were only milking parlours and funeral parlours and he doubted that I had either of those in mind.

Where the fireplace was concerned, however, I held my ground. Years earlier when we had demolished parts of the old house, I had rescued a cast-iron fireplace from Aunty Peg's bedroom upstairs and had stored it away in the attic, hoping that some day I would sit beside it and toast my toes. Now my hour had come. I coaxed one six-foot son to drag it out from under the attic dust and to bring it downstairs.

"What are you going to do with that heap of rubbish?" he demanded scornfully. Admittedly it did not look great, but I had high hopes for it.

Eventually all the dirty construction work was behind us and we rang Deaf Enterprises to bring back the furniture. When they arrived home, I hardly recognised them. Bill Brennan was dark and glossy with all his spare parts attached and, no matter what my sister had thought, he certainly looked stunning. He looked better than he had when we brought him home from the honeymoon, and I was only sorry that they could not have carried out the same restoration job on me. The night we installed the restored fireplace I smiled with satisfaction when I saw the look of amazement on my son's face. I sat down beside it and looked around at all my old friends in their new coats and sighed with delight that everything had turned out according to plan.

I will always be grateful to Biddy for standing in judgment on my window, because she fanned a flickering flame into a blaze of action.

THE CORNER PRESS

Slowly, tediously,
Dead layers of paint
Are scraped away,
A technicolour combination
Of many coats.
Then rebirth,
Pale skin
Of the original
Comes through.
A wonderous moment
When she stands naked
In her pine perfection.

A Place for Miss Carter

O N A BRIGHT sunny summer's morning, I sat in the kitchen wondering whether I should drag myself upstairs to do some hoovering or yield to temptation to go out into the garden on the pretence of doing some gardening, but actually to get away from housework. The kitchen door burst open and my friend John from outside the village rushed in with an absorbed look on his face.

"I need you badly," he announced.

"It's nice to feel needed," I told him.

"Don't be funny," he warned me. "I have serious business on hand."

"Like what?" I demanded.

"I must find a grave for a body," he told me.

"Where did you find the body?" I asked in amazement.

"Sit down and I'll tell you the whole story, but put on the kettle first and we'll have a cup of tea while we discuss strategy."

"John," I told him, "people disposing of bodies don't have time to have cups of tea."

"Ah," he said, "there is no hurry that way. There is

154

one thing about the dead: they have more patience than the living."

"And where is that patient body waiting?" I asked.

"In London," he told me.

"But where do we come into the story?"

"Sit down now," he said, "and while we are having the tea I'll try to explain the whole story, and don't interrupt me because you'll confuse me and I have only barely got the story clear in my own head."

"Right," I said, "off with you."

"Well, this is it," he started: "A woman died in London a few days ago."

"I'd say a lot of women died in London a few days ago," I interpolated.

"Don't interrupt," he cautioned, and continued. "This woman had no family and apparently no relatives, but she had left instructions with her solicitor that when she died she wanted to be buried with her mother. Now, her mother was from Kinsale and the solicitor assumed that she was buried there, so yesterday he contacted the Kinsale clergy. They checked things out the best way they could and they think that the family grave is not in Kinsale."

"And what has all this got to do with us?" I wanted to know.

"Well, the undertaker talked with an old woman in Kinsale who thinks that the Carter family are buried in Innishannon."

"Ah," I said, "that poses a problem."

"Yes," he said, "we must find the grave."

"But how did you get involved?" I asked.

"I know the undertaker and he rang me," he said.

"He didn't by any chance know if it was the old or the new graveyard? Though you could hardly call the new graveyard new, as it is over a hundred years old, so she could easily be buried there as well."

"He had no idea," John said.

"Well," I decided, "there are a lot of possibilities, so we had better start a process of elimination. We'll start with the new graveyard."

Such a grand sunny morning was ideal for a walk about our restful graveyard, which is spread out around the church at the top of the hill. However, as I had half expected, there was no headstone with a Carter name on it. Having spent many evenings cutting the grass with a group of locals, I already had a fair idea who was resting in every corner. Local farmers with scythes used to come in after milking the cows to cut the grass, and many of their families had lived here for generations, so not only did they know each family grave, but they told interesting stories about them as they cleaned around the headstones.

"Well, she is not here anyway," I told John.

"Except she could be under one of those marking stones," he answered. The marking stones were just big pointed stones sticking up through the ground with nothing written on them; they were used before headstones.

"Somehow I have a feeling that it's down below

she is," I told him, referring to the old graveyard at the end of the village.

So we went down through the village to the old graveyard which surrounds the tower at the end of the village. Lying beneath the wood on the bank of the river, it is a peaceful place for the repose of bones at the end of life.

"Now where on earth would one start to look here?" John demanded as he looked around at the tilted headstones and sagging tombs. We took a side of the graveyard each and worked systematically back and forth.

A few hours later we met back at the base of the tower, with two blank faces.

"Nothing doing," John declared.

"She must be under the marking stones," I decided.

"We'll never find her there," John despaired as he gazed around the rows of marking stones scattered around the mounded graveyard at both sides of the old tower.

"Let's sit down," I said, "and review the situation."

So we sat down on a low tomb and tried to figure out the next step.

"How old is the Miss Carter who is dead?" I asked John.

"No idea," he said, "but somehow I gather that she was fairly old. So let's say that she was eighty, just to give us a guideline."

"Now, we will assume that her mother lived until

Miss Carter was an adult, which she probably did. That would mean that her funeral was here within the last fifty or sixty years, give or take a decade or two."

"Some of the old people around should remember that," John decided.

"But will they remember where?" I asked, looking at the wild state of the old graveyard, which was lovely in its own way but did not exactly provide a military row of precise records.

"We'd better have tea at this stage," John decided. "Grave-hunting is thirsty work."

As we drank our tea we discussed our problem with my husband Gabriel, who because he had lived in the village shop all his life knew everybody, and knew who amongst them possessed the best memories. He advised us to start with Billy in the forge.

Billy downed tools and scratched his head when we introduced him to our problem.

"Carter! Carter!" he repeated, as if to jog his memory. "They weren't farmers or horsey people, anyway, though I have a vague memory of the name in the village." The horse that Billy had been shoeing stamped his hoof restlessly on the stone floor as his young owner looked at us, obviously wondering had we nothing better to be doing than delaying Billy.

"Let it with me," Billy said, "and something might come back to me."

As we left the forge I asked John how long we had to find a resting place for Miss Carter.

"She is flying into Cork airport tonight," he said,

"and the burial is supposed to be tomorrow."

"I hope that they'll have somewhere to bury her," I said. "When do they plan to dig the grave?"

"This evening," he answered.

"That undertaker must have great faith in you," I said. "Where to next?"

"Let's try Ger," he said.

Ger lived alone in a farmhouse overlooking the village; as our parish poet, he recorded many local happenings in song and because he had a great memory was a sound source of local reference. When we called he was playing the violin and gave us an impromptu concert; Ger was a fine singer who liked to accompany himself on either the piano or the violin. A talented man who found fulfilment in writing and music, he farmed as a sideline.

Ger was immediately interested in our story.

"The Carters," he said to himself again and again, as if knocking on the door of his subconscious and hoping to awaken a memory. Suddenly he punched the palm of one hand with his fist.

"I have it!" he declared. "There were Carters living up Chapel Hill when I was going to school."

"Any more about them?" I asked hopefully.

"The daughter was a nice-looking girl," he said, with a smile on his face.

Our Miss Carter was beginning to take shape.

"Can't remember any more off the top of my head," he said, "but call back again and I'll have put on my thinking cap."

Our next port of call was Ernest, who had an interest in the history and people of the place. As we drove over to meet him, I recalled the first time I had become aware of his talents. Some Americans had called into our shop to trace their ancestral roots, but they had drawn a blank with me. Ernest had come into the shop for groceries and was standing nearby.

"Ernest," I asked, after introducing him to the Americans, "this lady's ancestors were Higgins from around here, but there are none of that family name here now. Have you any suggestions?"

"There is an old man called Higgins living alone away up at the other end of the parish, and I think that a lot of his ancestors went to America," Ernest told them. They were absolutely delighted. It was a breakthrough in their search that had up to then been going nowhere. They wanted to take a gift to the old man when they went to visit and looked for suggestions.

"A bottle of whiskey," Ernest told them.

When they had gone on their way, Ernest said to me, "Whether they find their ancestors or not they'll have a great evening with Tade, and by the time they have the bottle drank, they'll all be related."

The following morning the Americans called back to see me, delighted with their visit to Tade, and insisted that I listen to a tape of Tade telling them stories. On one of the tapes Tade told a story about a visit he had made to London and how one of his nephews had taken him to a strip club. It was a very funny story and the Americans laughed heartily as they listened to it. I asked them if they had ever met anybody like Tade.

"Never," they told me; "if we had him in America, we'd make him Mayor of New York."

When I recounted the story to Ernest, he smiled and said, "I knew that when Tade saw the bottle of whiskey he'd grow roots in all directions. There is no way of knowing but that they were the real thing."

As we drove in to Ernest's yard, I hoped that he might solve this problem as easily.

"Carter," he said, "now let me think. There was a little man called Carter living up Chapel Hill when I was going to school."

"That's right," I said, "Ger remembered that as well and that the daughter was good-looking."

"Trust Ger to remember that," he laughed.

"Could they be buried down in the old grave-yard?" I asked.

"Could be," he said thoughtfully. "Do you know now, the man to tell you that is Jim. His father used to look after that place when I was a boy and Jim spent a lot of time down there with him."

So we made our way to Jim's house, which was down the road on the river. He was out at the door to meet us.

"I was expecting ye," he laughed. "Called over to Billy earlier on and we were discussing it after ye had left."

"Did you come up with anything?" I asked.

"Well, now," he said, rubbing his hands, "this is a tricky one. There was a Carter man in the village long ago and he was a baker. Now, I don't think that he was from the village; I think that it was the wife who was from here." He tapped his walking stick off the floor, as if checking off his facts, as he went along.

He walked around in a circle with his eyes closed and said slowly, "They left the village – they weren't here that long actually – and I think that the wife was brought back to be buried here."

"In the old graveyard?" I asked.

"Oh, yes, of course," he said with no shadow of a doubt in his voice.

"Any idea where in the old graveyard?" John asked cautiously, almost afraid that if he rushed things he could disturb Jim's train of thought.

"Now, let me try to remember," he said, and I could nearly see his mind turning back the pages of his life. He screwed up his face in concentration and then he shook his head.

"I'd have to go down there now to have it come back to me," he said.

"Right! Hop in," John said, opening the door of the car, though "hop in" would not exactly describe Jim's careful climb into the front seat.

When we arrived at the old graveyard, Ernest was there before us.

"Now," I said, "we have the experts here together."

"The Carters are buried at the right-hand side of the path," Jim said decisively.

"You're right there," Ernest agreed, "but where, is the question?"

They walked around the marking stones almost as if the feel of the ground would bring back forgotten memories.

"It could be somewhere around there," Jim said, pointing his stick at a mound of grass that had grown undisturbed for years.

"Maybe more to the front," Ernest decided.

"Yes," Jim agreed slowly.

"And after that your guess is as good as ours, but it's somewhere in that area," Ernest declared.

Later that evening I met the grave-diggers at the foot of the old tower.

"You know where the Carter grave is, I think?" the older of the two asked.

"Yes," I said more confidently than I felt. I walked over and pointed to a spot; at the same time I looked up to heaven and prayed silently.

"Lord, only you alone know if this is the right place, so please direct the shovels." The grave-diggers started their job and I walked back home through the village.

That night, before darkness had fallen, I returned to the old graveyard. Around the newly dug grave was a mound of rich brown earth. I stood there wondering about Miss Carter, hoping that she was going into her mother's grave as she had wished. Then I saw, thrown sideways on the mound of earth, the corner of a coffin plate. I stooped down and wiped the fresh earth off. The name on it was "Carter".

The following day she arrived into the old grave-yard accompanied by a priest and the undertaker; birds sang in welcome. When she was laid to rest, John and I placed a bunch of wild flowers on her grave. Her wish to be buried with her mother was granted with the help of both local and divine intervention.

WALKING IT OFF

BEFORE I OPENED my eyes, I knew that I had slept it out. Living as we do on the side of the hill leading up to the school and within hearing distance of the main road, we learn to gauge the time of day from the traffic sounds.

There was no great traffic on the hill, so that meant that the school cars were gone, and as well as that the morning had a late feel about it. I opened one eye and looked at the alarm clock on the bedside table. It was ten o'clock. I closed my eyes again and sank down under the bedclothes, hoping that the day would go away. The previous days had seen a writing blitz late into the night, and now every muscle along the back of my neck ached in protest and my mind had gone on strike.

I was surprised that nobody had put their head around the door to see if I was dead or alive. I thought of a friend who maintained that he could be dead for three days and if he did not have the keys of the family car in his pocket nobody would miss him.

Then I decided that I needed a day off. Once the

decision was made, the day took on a whole new meaning. It was an occasion to be welcomed with open arms. I jumped out of the bed and looked into the mirror, only to recoil in horror at the image that confronted me. I recalled the occasion a few years previously when I had been going through a painting epidemic. So filled had I been with oil paint fever that I had withdrawn into the attic for days to the detriment of the house and all and sundry. One evening my sister called to be met by a greasy-haired, paint-spotted derelict. Sternly she informed me that I was going to seed.

If she were to see me now, her remark might not even be as kind. So I withdrew into the bathroom and emerged an hour later a new model to all outward appearances, but still in the need of internal restoration.

I did not even look into the kitchen for fear that I might see jobs waiting to be done. Instead I sneaked out the side door and up the hill with no specific destination in mind. The hill was steep so I was puffing when I reached the top, but once there the wind got behind me and helped me on my way. It blew my hair in all directions and the cobwebs out of my head and whipped my blood into circulation. I began to feel alive.

There is nothing like a walk on a windy day, and I will always be grateful to the friend who told me that walking releases the "happy" hormones. As I arrived at the first crossroads, the wind made the decision of which road to take. We blew along together and I could feel the relaxation creep across the back of my shoulders.

After a few miles I found myself at the back gate of St Patrick's Upton, a home for adult mentally handicapped people who are cared for by Rosminian priests and Drishane nuns. Many of "the lads", as they are known locally, live in bungalows around the grounds with house-parents in charge, and some are in the main unit. It is a large complex with many workshops and a farm attached, and some of the lads are trained to help in the workshops. Some of them are better able to cope than others, and a few months previously four of them had moved into the back lodge where they were living on their own, with an eye kept on them from the main house. The lad in charge, Joe, had several times invited me for tea in his new home.

Now I looked in over the hedge and saw that they were sitting inside the window having tea. I pushed open the small black gate and walked up the narrow path between two neat green lawns. I had always loved this little lodge, with its small, deep windows and high-pitched roof. Before I had time to knock, Joe opened the door with a big warm welcoming smile on his face.

"Come in, come in," he said. "You're just in time for the tea, but I'll show you our house first."

It was like a birds' nest. To the left of their small front hall was a comfortable sitting-room with easy chairs and a warm fire and to the right their fitted kitchen where they were eating. In the corner an old-fashioned high stairs led up into two bedrooms, which were fitted out with twin beds and every facility they could need. Behind their kitchen was an open utility area and a large bathroom. Joe opened the back door and led me across a little yard to a small house which held a washing machine and tumble-dryer, with which they could do their own laundry. Joe was as proud as Punch of his new living quarters and so were his companions.

One of the lads was called Noel and he had Down's syndrome. I had known his mother many years before, and her one worry had always been Noel's future: he was an only child, so there were no brothers or sisters to help out. She had worried about what would become of him when she and her husband were gone. As I watched him, so happy in this comfortable corner, I thought that she could not have wanted more for him.

It was obvious that Joe was the man in charge as he poured out tea and cut cake for the others. Sitting around the table with them was like going back into the uncomplicated world of childhood; they had no expectations of me, and in life that is a rare enough experience. As I walked along the avenue afterwards I felt strangely soothed by their company.

The wind bent the avenue of trees before it, the branches waved in protest and I was almost blown around a corner into the courtyard between the tall buildings. I was glad to close the back door of the monastery behind me. Inside it was quiet with an echo of distant voices. There is always in Upton an air of great order, and even though it houses over a hundred mentally handicapped, it still gives the impression of being a family home. It runs on the oiled wheels of good organisation and the welfare of the people in care is the first priority. No matter what hour of the day or night one walks through Upton, Bob, who has been here for as long as I can remember, will put his head out through some door or window to say hello. Now, as I put my foot on the bottom step of the stairs, he popped his head out through a door down the corridor and called up to me, "Alice, you're mad to be out in this weather."

"Bob," I told him, "I like a stormy day."

"You're going up to the prayer room," he said.

The small prayer room, boasting only a tabernacle in the corner and a few chairs and praying stools, was enveloped in the sound of silence. When I opened the door, I saw Fr Jim sitting on a chair with his legs on a stool and his eyes closed, a picture of total relaxation. He was on his lunch break and having a few minutes' communication with his boss. Hearing the door he opened his eyes and grinned up at me, his dark face full of merriment. Neither of us spoke because this room was all about silence. It took me a while to adjust myself, but gradually I wound down. I knew by the regular breathing from Fr Jimmy's chair that he had drifted off to sleep, and the same thing must have happened to me, because when I looked at his chair again he was gone. As always in this room I was reminded, "Be still and know that I am God."

As I walked down the front avenue on my way home, I met one of the lads who told me that he was going picking sticks. It was something that we had always done as children, but it was a long time since I had met anybody doing it in recent times. We sauntered together chatting and parted at the gate, he to the wood and I on the road home.

Coming down the hill back into the village, the grey-white church steeple towered over the dark trees and welcomed me back. It had been a grand walk and I felt that all my happy hormones had been released.

A Sudsy Soak

Swirls of steam
Wrap my tired body;
An old, old woman,
Whom nobody loves.
I crawl feebly
Over the bath edge
And submerge into
The sudsy warmth.
My body dissolves,
My mind evaporates;
I become nothing,
Drifting into oblivion.
A few hot water top-ups
And an hour later
I come back together.
It's good to be alive,
Everybody loves me
And I high-step
Out of the bath,
Vibrant and beautiful,
And the old lady
With all her problems
Disappears down
The plug-hole.

ON AIR

MY HUSBAND TURNED the key in the ignition and the engine gave a long, soft growl like a dog who had no intention of getting off his backside. He tried again and the growl grew fainter.

"Blast it," he said between gritted teeth, and I silently echoed his sentiment. He tried again and again and the whirr grew fainter and fainter.

"We'll take Mike's car," Gabriel decided, in a tone of voice that did not invite comment.

"Oh God," I thought, "the wheels could fall off it half-way to Dublin." But it was no time for open and frank discussion, so I swallowed my misgivings.

Gabriel was already at the wheel of our son's sports model, which roared into action like a young lion. The sound brought our son's head out of an upstairs window.

"Where are you going with my car?" he demanded of his father.

"To Dublin," he was told sternly.

If Mike did not like the idea, neither did his mother. But my concerns about having to drive a strange car when Gabriel got tired were the least of my worries.

Earlier that morning I had woken up to find my nine-year-old daughter by my bed.

"Alice," she had whispered, "the birds are awake." And sure enough the dawn chorus was just starting, and as I listened for a few seconds, I thought that this would be a lovely day, but then my brain cleared and reality hit me like a cold shower.

"Oh, Mother of God," I groaned, "the Gay Byrne Show!"

"That's why I called you," my daughter said practically; "it's time to get up."

"Len," I implored her, "will you say a prayer for me today that I don't drop down stone-cold dead on live radio?"

"You'll be all right," she assured me comfortingly. "Mildred Anne will take care of you."

It had taken my sleep-muddled and terror-stricken brain a few seconds to work that one out. Mildred Anne Butler was the artist who had painted the threshing scene on the cover of the book which I was going to talk about on the radio show. She had gone on to heavenly scenes, but the thought that she could be with me in spirit had seemed strangely comforting.

Nobody was to be seen as we drove down through our village; the only sign of life was a black dog in the middle of the road scratching behind his ear with his back leg. He was so intent on relieving his itch that Gabriel had to drive around him, which did nothing for my husband's already frayed patience.

We left Cork behind and drove along the quiet, early morning roads. I tried to brainwash myself into forgetting the ordeal ahead, to concentrate on the sun lighting up the Galtees and to admire the colour variations of the summer trees. Normally I love long-distance driving early in the morning when the countryside is fresh and the dew is glistening, but on that particular morning my concentration span cracked every few minutes as I remembered what lay ahead. I had never before been on live radio and the prospect gave me mental paralysis. At least, I comforted myself, people won't be able to see me. All I will have to do is open my mouth. But then, I thought, maybe no sound will come out. The first croaking, gasping interviewee on radio! A Natterjack toad being interviewed! Then I tried to convince myself that maybe nobody might be listening anyway. I had told nobody in the village that I was going to be on and had warned my children to tell nobody, at least until I was gone to Dublin.

Mike had said, "You're crazy! How do you think that you can be on the Gay Byrne Show and nobody hear you? The whole country listens to that."

One side of my addled brain knew that he was right, but in some strange way I felt that if my friends and neighbours did not know that I was going to be on, they would have no expectations of me and then no matter what kind of a mess I made of it I would not feel so bad about it.

We were making great headway on the quiet roads and I comforted myself with the thought that at least we would have plenty of time to find RTÉ. I had located the radio station on a map, but I was not the most accomplished of navigators, having been known in the past to finish up in places far from the proposed destination. Beside me Gabriel was silent and intent on his driving, his nose a little out of joint after being let down by his own car.

Suddenly he swore, "That bloody fool!"

I looked around but there was not another motorist in sight.

"What bloody fool?" I asked in confusion.

"Mike!" he said in exasperation.

Getting no reaction from his dim-witted wife, he pointed to the petrol gauge. I turned my eyes in horrified fascination to where his finger was doing a barn dance on the glass in front of a small black pointer that was well down into the red section.

"Sons!" I thought. "There should be a law against them. They never have full petrol tanks, and if they get a loan of your car, it always comes back full of thirst."

Straight away I decided that I could not afford to indulge in the luxury of panic. I remembered reading somewhere that if you were going to talk on radio a prior period of calm was absolutely necessary. So panic was out of the question. Meanwhile my husband was rehearsing what he planned to say to his first-born when he got home that night.

"We must not get excited now," I said, which of course was the wrong thing to say.

"Who is getting excited?" he asked tetchily.

I decided to try a more meaningful tactic.

"What are we going to do?"

"Find petrol," he stated grimly.

We were out on the open road without a house, not to mind a petrol station, in sight. "Mildred Anne," I asked silently, "where are you now?" I had thought that I would not need help until my arrival in the studio, but things were going wrong ahead of schedule. Suddenly a small town loomed on the horizon and I felt like shouting "Land Ahoy!" Where there is a town there is usually a petrol station, but there are exceptions to that rule and this was one.

We continued, and suddenly we were rewarded by the sight of pumps in the distance. The closed sign glared at us, but I felt that we could not be this near to petrol and not be able to get at it. I was wrong. We knocked on the doors and we blew the horn but the whole place was like a graveyard. Valuable time was ticking away, so we decided to take a calculated risk and continue. As we drove out of that petrol station I felt like a man on a desert island when a liner passes by on the horizon.

At this point I was wondering if Gay Byrne had plenty of records to put on when guests failed to turn up. I could understand then why the producer had wanted me to stay in Dublin the night before.

But of course I had known better and had wanted to come up from home in the morning.

As we drove along, expecting that any minute the car would grind to a halt, I could feel tension crawl up the back of my neck. Then I got a brainwave: I would do my yoga exercises. At home I did them to the sound of a tape on the floor of an upstairs attic, but now I decided that I would do them in my mind. I closed my eyes and recalled the soothing voice on the tape saying slowly: "You are lying in the corpse position, so you should be nicely relaxed and ready to begin your yoga session".

It took great mental concentration to block out the present trauma and to imagine myself relaxed on the attic floor listening to the velvety voice of the instructor, and just when I was almost there, a voice far from velvety jolted me back.

"What's wrong with you? Are you sick?"

Another town appeared on the horizon and the first house at the edge of it was a garda barracks.

"We'll ask here," Gabriel decided; "they always know the lie of the land."

Sure enough, the tall, heavy guard who answered our knock stretched his arms above his sleepy head and said, "A few miles down the road is a garage that will be opening in about twenty minutes. Have you enough to get there?"

We prayed that we had, and as we crawled into that station, I felt a load lift off my shoulders. But with the solving of one problem, we became more aware of our second one. We were now running out of time. Leaving the petrol station, I clung to my seat as Gabriel put his foot down.

I was imagining Gay Byrne's voice announcing on radio, "Alice Taylor, who has just published her first book, was to have appeared on this show this morning, but unfortunately they are now scraping her off the Naas dual carriageway."

Eventually we arrived in the suburbs of Dublin and I took over, giving frantic directions to Donnybrook. When I saw water-hens swimming serenely on the canal, I envied them their tranquility in the midst of traffic bedlam. For a fleeting moment, a picture of the little river we used to cross over on our way to school flashed across my mind, but I was jerked back to reality by a terse voice.

"Where next?"

"Turn right here," I instructed.

"There is no right turn here!"

I stared in horror at the no entry sign.

"Mother of God," I thought, "will anything go right this morning?"

"Well, there is a right turn on the map," I insisted.

"We're not driving on the map."

"You're on your own, so," I told him, throwing the map on to the back seat.

Gabriel's in-built sense of direction took over and eventually we spotted a sign for Donnybrook. But finding RTÉ remained a problem.

"Look out for a mast," Gabriel instructed; "there

must be a high mast in RTÉ."

I put my head down and craned it forward like a goose drinking water and peered out through the windscreen to view the chimney-tops of Dublin. Then I tried the back window, but the bearded man in the car close behind gave me a baleful stare. Not a mast in sight! We were crawling at a snail's pace through early morning traffic and my blood pressure was clocking red like the patrol gauge earlier on. My desirable period of calm prior to going on radio was well and truly shattered. The minutes were ticking by, reaching ever closer to the time I had been instructed to present myself in RTÉ.

Then suddenly I spotted a mast and it was like manna in the desert.

"It's over there!" I shouted.

"Where?" Gabriel demanded.

"Over there," I said, pointing vaguely.

"You should have been a ship's captain," he told me; "maybe your sense of direction would have been better at sea."

But I knew that we were headed in the right direction when he made a fast turn towards where I had seen the mast, and then we could both see it without dislocating our necks.

"I hope to God this is not just a telephone exchange," I said as we drove in the unmarked gate.

"Is this RTE?" I asked the surprised security guard.

"Well, where do you think you are?" he smiled and directed us to the radio centre.

I jumped out of the car and ran up the steps just on the dot of the time that I had been told to be there. As I collapsed into a chair in the lobby, the researcher arrived.

"You are not on for a while yet."

I sighed with relief at the prospect of having time to gather my thoughts and achieve some semblance of calm. But before I had time to relax and gather my wits, another girl dashed in waving a sheaf of papers in the air.

"Come on," she ordered, "change of plans: you're on now!" And she ran off down a long corridor with me hot on her heels. At the end of the corridor, she opened a grey door into a tiny, windowless cell and I saw at last the object of my journey, Gay Byrne, seated at a large table with wires sprouting out of his head. Panting a little, I sat into a chair at the table, and almost before I knew it the interview had begun. For all the hectic anxiety of the drive, I was so relieved to have arrived that I forgot to be worried.

ROSE

OSE HAD ALWAYS worn a harassed look. She had her hands full with small children and a husband who was not exactly helpful around the house, and her mother-in-law, who drove her bananas, was for ever dropping in. Although I could understand why she looked that way, I often felt irritated by Rose's lonesome expression, and I became fed up listening to her sad stories. Often I felt like telling her to pull herself together but held back for fear of hurting her feelings.

Then gradually, almost without my actually noticing it at first, Rose started to change. The complaining dried up and she started to smile. It puzzled me slightly but I was slow to comment on it in case, like a bright bubble in the air, it might disappear. But it continued and the bubble got bigger and brighter. Then I decided that she must be having an affair: she had fallen in love and that was the reason for the glow. If I had been married to her cranky, selfish husband, I thought, I would have been having an affair as well.

She never said a word but continued to cope

happily with little things that she had previously complained about non-stop. I waited cynically for the bubble to burst, calculating that if an affair was involved, somebody would make a decisive move at some stage. I was terrified that Rose would get hurt in the fall-out, and then we would be back to square one. However, she made no reference to any-thing unusual happening in her life and I could not imagine where she fitted in time for her affair. Then I tried to think whether she had been going anywhere different over the last few months, and realised that the only outing she had taken up recently was going to a prayer meeting in Upton. That, I thought, could hardly be the cause of the change in her; after all, Rose was no Bible-carrying, born-again Christian.

Then one day she asked me to go with her.

"A prayer meeting?" I queried dubiously. "That doesn't exactly appeal to me. What do you do there? Wave your hands in the air and sit around chanting alleluia?"

She threw back her head and laughed: "What gave you that daft notion?"

"I don't know," I admitted, "but I always had the idea that prayer group people were a bit over the top."

"Ah," she told me, "your prejudices are showing. Ours is a very normal, well-earthed crowd."

"Well, you're like that anyway," I admitted.

"Why don't you come and see for yourself?" she invited. "The only way you will find out is to come and see for yourself. You are the person who is always telling me that you must judge every situation for yourself and here you are telling me about something that I know all about and you know nothing about."

I hesitated to take Rose up on her suggestion, feeling that prayer was a private thing that needed silence and peace and quiet. Rose, however, was very persistent, and I wondered could this possibly be the explanation for the change in her. So, as much out of curiosity as anything else, I set out for Upton the following Monday night.

I was not impressed by my first experience of a prayer meeting. Surrounded by people deep in meditation, I felt uncomfortable, even claustrophobic.

Afterwards, while we shared a cup of tea, a friend of Rose's remarked, "Don't judge on the first night; come again next week and give it a chance."

I murmured something non-committal, but thought to myself that once was quite enough.

For most of the week that followed, I thought no more about the prayer meeting, but for no special reason that I could put my finger on, I felt a certain inner peace. Out walking early one sunny morning, I watched a hare racing through a meadow while all around me the air was rich with the smell of wild woodbine. The beauty of the whole scene made me consider the glory of creation, made me wonder about the presence of God in nature, and turned my thoughts back to the prayer meeting. As Monday night approached, I experienced a sense of curiosity.

That night I felt less self-conscious in the silence. I relaxed and soon found myself in tune with the spirit of the meeting. A woman with a Northern Ireland accent read from the Bible and shared her thoughts on the reading; others joined in. It was quite spontaneous and nobody was under pressure to say or do anything that did not appeal to them. One young girl with a beautiful voice sang a hymn that I had never heard before. She sang it during a period of meditative silence and I sensed that it was completely unplanned.

I experienced at that meeting a great sense of togetherness in the presence of God, and over the following weeks it developed, the peace of the prayer meeting spreading out into other regions of my life. It seemed almost as though at Upton those two hours of meditation every Monday night provided a powerhouse into which I could plug myself. Now life ran much more smoothly, and not only had I discovered Rose's secret, I had discovered something of my own.

Book Signing

THE OLD MAN'S face was kind and his skin like fine beige tissue-paper stretched tautly across protruding bones; there was no hairline to show where face ended and head began. Over his ears and around the back of his poll the last remnants of his hair fell gently in a downy white frill. A threadbare tweed jacket with leather elbow patches hung loosely on his angular frame and cavalry twill trousers held up by gigantic braces encompassed his long legs, which I imagined to be thin and bony. His leather boots of many creases shone with a dark, rich shine from years of polishing. The whole harmonious colour scheme of muted browns was sparked into life by his bright yellow shirt and deep red cravat. He held out his hand and I put mine into it, warmed by the merriment that sparkled in his dark brown eyes. His hand felt dry and brittle and I almost expected it to crinkle like autumn leaves between my fingers. "Heard you've written a great book, my dear," he said in a voice that was surprisingly deep and rich in so frail a body.

"Hope you'll like it," I answered.

"Could be interesting, old thing," he answered, leaving me unsure whether it was the book or myself was the "old thing".

"Never did go to school through the fields, you know. Always had a governess. Bloody awful women, some of them! But one had to put up with them. Anyway, the body might like it," he concluded.

I digested this statement for a few seconds hoping that he might add something further to throw light on "the body".

"I am the body," said a tall, elegant lady, stepping out from behind the tweedy form.

Some women are cool blondes at thirty but here was one at about seventy. With her flaring nostrils and high cheek-bones, she would be beautiful even in death.

"Had a terrific body, you know," he announced to all and sundry. "Not bad still, old girl," he added, grinning wickedly at her. She took it serenely in her stride.

Suddenly from the back of the queue came a high-pitched crackling voice, which demanded in domineering tones, "George, for God's sake, will you get a move on and don't be holding everything up."

George threw up his head like a well-bred race-horse and peered back over the line of people.

"Hello! Molly old girl!" he called back. "Never could wait for anything could you? That's why you were so bloody awful with horses... And men," he added under his breath. Before she could retaliate, he picked up his book and together with his beautiful wife swept towards the door, making an exit with flourish and style.

Next in the queue was a gentle-faced woman with wavy auburn hair who made a couple of attempts to say something, but at the last minute changed her mind. Just as she was about to move on, it came out.

"Did you never think of dying your hair?" she asked. "Your face looks much younger than your hair."

As I put my hand up protectively towards my greying thatch, she added apologetically: "I don't mean to offend you, now. It is just that it would make you look much younger."

I assured her that it would take more than that to offend me and that the only reason my hair was going grey was because I was too lazy to do anything about it, and as well as that I rather liked grey hair. Somehow she did not look very reassured by my excuses and went away convinced, I thought, that I was an old hag going to seed.

As they queued the people chatted and exchanged remembrances; old friends met each other with great delight. Even though I was the one they had come to meet, I was finding them fascinating to watch and to listen to. Some when their turns came were reluctant to part with new-found friends and made arrangements to meet again, sometimes filling me in on all they had in common. The queue had developed into a small party and little groups formed to discuss items of interest in the book. People who had come into the shop in a hurry, all of a sudden had all the time in the world. But if they spent too much time chatting with me, the manager would hover restlessly beside them, hoping to hurry things up a bit.

One woman dressed all in dramatic black, including a black veil, was particularly talkative. When the manager attempted gently to encourage her on her way, she swept up her black veil and announced imperiously: "Young man, I did not come here to be rushed. Please desist!"

He bowed to her command, and who was I to do otherwise?

A jovial priest beamed at me next. "You are the first woman ever to share my bed," he announced. "It was three o'clock this morning before I put you under my pillow."

We talked for a few minutes about childhood experiences and if we had had the time could have chatted for hours, so full of fun and yarns was he. Molly, however, was close on his heels and stamped her walking stick with annoyance.

"The old bird behind will hit me a belt of her stick if I don't get a move on," he whispered, and he ran out the door with the book under his arm and the bounce of a much younger man in his step.

At last Molly had me at her mercy. Two beady eyes peered at me from either side of a hawk-like nose and red hair streaked with grey swung to her shoulders. Looking at Molly I thought that my caring lady earlier on could have been right. Maybe grey hair did not look very elegant. But if Molly did not look elegant, she certainly looked interesting. Wrapped in a long grey coat, she sparkled with jewellery. Neck, ears, fingers and wrists were ablaze and if they were the real thing, which they possibly were, she carried a walking fortune.

"No book," she announced, tapping her walking stick off the floor, "is worth this much trouble. My fool of a husband Roger insisted that I get a copy. Can't imagine why. Went to a private school himself so what the hell does he know about going to school through the fields. Couldn't come himself. Oh no! Can't stand with his bloody gout. But I tell him if you drink that damn stuff you can't expect anything else."

"Do you want something special written on it," I ventured to distract her from her monologue.

She threw back her head and roared with laughter.

"Put 'To Roger, You silly old fool, From Cuddles'. That will teach him not to send me doing his errands. He'll be furious because he won't be able to loan it to his old drinking cronies."

As I handed her the book, she patted my hand with a ringed bony finger.

"Don't mind me, my dear," she said, smiling mischievously and revealing remnants of the beauty that she must once have been but, unlike "the body", had made no effort to preserve.

"Goodbye, you clever girl," she said, adding, "I'll

probably read it too." And she walked to the door, stick tapping and jewellery flashing.

After Molly a large lady breathed heavily down upon me.

"I could have written that book myself," she informed me, "only I hadn't the time. Writing is all right for people who have nothing better to be doing."

The queue had now dwindled and a trickle of people came along with whom I discussed their childhoods and the pros and cons of modern life. Then in front of me stood a little man with wisps of grey standing up all over his head and eyes sparkling behind rimless glasses.

"The only girl who ever asked me to marry her came from your home town," he announced.

"And did you marry her?" I asked.

"No," he answered, "because she frightened the pants off me."

An unfortunate choice of words, I thought, but he proceeded merrily.

"She was one of those progressive thinkers and was way ahead of her time and certainly ahead of my thinking."

"Where did you meet?" I asked.

"We were going to university together. She did medicine and, when she qualified, went to England. Never met her since," he concluded wistfully.

"And did you get married afterwards?" I asked to bring back the smile to his face.

"Oh yes," he said brightening up, "and had four children," he added firmly as if to prove to himself that he really did.

"But do you know something?" he asked confidentially, looking into my eyes as if somewhere in there was the spirit of his old love, "I sometimes think of that grand girl and hope that she never lost her free spirit."

I watched him walk away. A little man in a grey suit, and no one would ever guess that he carried a lost dream within.

My afternoon signing books was almost over, but I felt enriched by the lives of the many people who had shared their memories and idiosyncrasies with me. They had come to hear my story but each one of them had their own story, some ordinary and some extraordinary, and sometimes in life the ordinary can be extraordinary.